MW00892790

DON'T STRUGGLE BECOME YOUR STANDARD

HOW TO BE

INDISPENSABLE

EVEN WHEN THE ODDS ARE STACKED AGAINST YOU

JOSE FLORES

FOREWARD BY LES BROWN

Don't Let Your Struggle Become Your Standard

By: Jose Flores

No part of this book may be reproduced in any form or by any electronic or mechanical means, including photocopying, recording, or by any informational storage and retrieval systems, without permission in writing from the author, except by reviewers, who may quote brief passages in a review.

Book QR videos by: PV Creative

Book cover design by: Luner Eugene

Book cover photo by: Lisandro Fernandez

Books may be purchased in quantity and/or special sales by contacting the author Jose Flores at 305-563-4634 or via email at joseinspires@gmail.com

Visit: www.joseinspires.com

Copyright © 2017 JOSE FLORES
All rights reserved.

ISBN- 13: 9781976554544
ISBN- 10: 1976554543

What People Are Saying about Don't Let Your Struggle Become Your Standard

"Jose Flores is an inspiration, not only in terms of his words, but more importantly in terms of his actions. This book will lift your thinking and your spirits!"

Dr. Willie Jolley, Host of the #1 Inspirational Radio Show on *Sirius XM* and Best Selling Author of *"A Setback Is A Setup For A Comeback."*

"Inspiring, Authentic, and Motivating! Jose is a powerful voice for anyone who wants to overcome and dominate adversity physically, emotionally, or psychologically. A great read!"

Dr. Jada Jackson, Licensed Mental Health Counselor. Life Coach, Author of *Be-You-Tiful* and Talk Show Host of *Emotional Mojo.*

"A required reading for anyone that has experienced a major setback in life and is looking for a way forward. Jose does this through personal anecdotes, which is a highly effective way of giving the reader perspective. He embodies the lesson that no one should be defined by circumstances beyond their control."

David Hernandez, CEO and Co-Founder, Liberty Power Corp

DEDICATION

This book is dedicated to

My best friend and the woman of my dreams,
my beautiful wife Andrea Flores:

You love me unconditionally, you motivate me beyond measure, you are always there for me through thick and thin, and you always push me to reach my maximum potential. You are truly my helpmate and the love of my life. I am so blessed to call you my wife and so glad that I get to share this amazing life with the most beautiful woman on the planet. I wouldn't be who I am today without you by my side. You make me better than I am. I love you honey!

To our sons Elijah and Zion:

You two are the best children parents could ever ask for. You both are intelligent, strong, funny, kind, caring, and most importantly very loving. I am so proud of you both and the great men you are becoming. I thank you for all your love, support, and help, as I wouldn't be able to do all the things I do without you guys. I love you both very much and couldn't have asked for better children. I thank God every day for the family He has blessed me with.

CONTENTS

ACKNOWLEDGMENTS

To my parents Leon and Lourdes Santiago thank you for never giving up on me, loving me unconditionally and raising me to become a great husband, father, and friend. Thank you for encouraging me to always chase my dreams; if it weren't for you I wouldn't be living them today. Thank you for always keeping me in your prayers. I love you mom and dad!

To my mother-in-law Trina Olson for always helping out when we need you, being there for us and keeping us in prayer. I love and appreciate you tremendously Trina!

To my spiritual parent's Pastor's Tom and Candi Manning, thank you for your prayers, teachings, and impartation. Thank you for showing me what it is to be a true disciple of Christ and for helping me grow rapidly in my walk with Jesus. All I want to do is be a messenger of hope everywhere I go and to everyone I meet! I love and appreciate you both.

To Tito and Daniela Hernandez for being truly amazing friends and making sure that I'm always okay. You both rock! Love you!!

To my siblings and family members: My sisters Tyhisha Alamo, HopeRose Santiago, and Debbie Santiago, to my brothers Tyson Santiago, Eric Flores, and Jeffery Santiago. To my cousins: Mark Santiago, Richie (Boogie) Succi, and my amazing godmother Aida Torres. Thank you for all your love and support. Thank you for all the good times, memories, and for never treating me any differently. I love you all.

To my brothers from another mother who have always been there for me and stayed close to me for many years no matter how far or close we live: Emilio (Zeno) Baez, Jose (Tuti) Rodriguez, Oscar Colon, Ray Rincon, and Anibal (Junito) Irizarry. Thank you for literally carrying me on your backs, up and down the stairs for all those years, never judging me, and helping me to live my life to the fullest! I love you guys! Thank you to all my other friends and family who also gave me a helping hand, (or back LOL), there are too many to mention but you know who you are. Thank you!

To my mentor and friend Les Brown, words truly cannot express how thankful I am to have you in my life and for the relationship we've built. The wisdom, advice, and guidance you have shared with me are priceless! I am forever grateful. You saw my potential from the beginning. Thank you for believing in me, investing your time with me, and telling me to shoot for the moon!

To my Lord and Savior Jesus Christ for giving me the wisdom, strength, and endurance to finish this book and continue running my race for His glory! Thank you for protecting me and healing me. Thank you for your grace and your mercy. Thank you for using me, blessing me and having favor on me so that I can shine your light everywhere I go. Thank you Jesus! I definitely couldn't have done it without you. I love you with all my heart, mind, soul, and strength.

FOREWORD BY LES BROWN

S ocrates said, *"What lies behind us and what lies before us is of small consequence to what lies within us."* As you think about your life right now I want to say to you, as Jose would say, "You are absolutely necessary, you are indispensable." Jose is an author, he's a dynamic speaker, trainer, a husband, and father, and I'm proud to say my mentee. He has written a book that is a game changer. Jose is an incredible example that regardless of the adversities that life will throw at you, that they're of a small consequence to what's within you. Jose lives this every day of his life. As a dedicated individual to help people to live their dreams and to realize that their lives matter, in the scheme of things that you are indispensable, a message that is needed now more than ever before.

More people committed suicide in the United States of America than died from traffic accidents. Something is wrong with that. They have given up hope.

11

They don't realize that their lives are necessary and important. There is a reason for you being here. You are a masterpiece because you are a piece of the master. Jose in each page of this life-changing book proves beyond a reasonable doubt, that you have something special, that greater is He that is in you than he that is in the world, that you are more than a conqueror. Jose & I share the stage together encouraging people to live their dreams and because of our close relationship, he helps me to deal with cancer that I have been dealing with and fighting for 21 years, and the pain from sciatica. His example strengthens my faith every day to continue to live the calling on my life, in spite of, like he does. Jose, I'm proud of you and those of you that are reading this book, by the time you get to the last chapter, your life will never be the same!

That's my story and I'm sticking to it!

World Renowned Author and Motivational Expert
*~ **Les Brown***

INTRODUCTION

S truggles are one of those things that none of us are exempt from. However, all of us have the power to overcome them. The difference is; some *choose* to fight and push through their struggles and overcome, while others just tend to give up and settle for where they are in life and let it become their standard. For many, it may be financial, emotional, psychological, spiritual, or physical struggles. While for others it may be marital, relational, or social struggles.

Since you have decided to read this book you may be asking yourself, what about the struggles that may seem unbearable and can't be overcome? That's a great question. I had that same question when my wife Andrea and I first started dating. I thought that my struggle of being in a wheelchair would be unbearable for her to withstand and have to deal with. However, I am excited to let you know that this year we will be celebrating 10 years of being happily married and still going strong. Does overcoming any struggle take work, sacrifice, dedication, discipline, and commitment? Absolutely!

The question I have for you is this; will you do it? Will you sacrifice? Will you fight? Will you stay committed? Will you keep pressing forward? Will you overcome? Will you stay the course? Will you keep chasing your dreams until they become your reality? I believe that you have the willingness to do so and that your answer is yes. I believe that before you are done reading this book, you will be well on your way to living the Indispensable life now!

In this book, I will share with you strategies, stories, and experiences that will equip you and teach you how to become successful in overcoming any challenge in life even when the odds are stacked against you. My hope is that after reading this book, you will feel motivated and excited about going to the next level. I believe that once you start to understand that challenges are inevitable in life but being defeated by them is optional, you will become unstoppable.

I hope you enjoy the journey! Great things are on the horizon!

CHAPTER 1

How to Live and Be Indispensable Now

ave you ever felt undervalued or insignificant? Have you ever felt incapable or inadequate at any point in your life? I have at many times and the feeling is terrible. In this book, I am going to share with you ways to overcome adversity, unleash your greatness and maximize your full potential even when the odds are stacked against you.

I will show you that your current situation doesn't have to become your future reality. You were created to be Indispensable and I want to help show you how to tap into it and let loose the greatness that has been locked up inside of you.

What better time than now? What better moment than this? What are you waiting for? What is it that's holding you back? Now is the time my friends, to climb up and conquer the mountain that has been in your way for so long. Let the journey begin, spread your wings, and I'll see you at the top. Let's go!

The purpose of this book is to inspire, encourage, and empower you to release the fears that have been holding you back and keeping you from maximizing your full potential for so many years. If you are somewhat like me, then you will understand as you continue reading that it is time to live a life that is Indispensable Now. You can live an Indispensable Now life by embracing the amazing greatness that already lives inside of you today! Many of us go through life with feelings of insignificance, inadequacy, and being incapable of achieving success on a higher level. My goal is to help you navigate through those emotions and feelings. Also, for you to understand that there is a purpose for you, there is a plan for your life, and that you were created for an abundant living! We will get into purpose and passion a little later on.

Sometimes the journey can be a little shaky. You lose control and you don't know which direction you should be going, what decisions you should be making, or if you even have what it takes to move forward. I'm here to tell you that I believe that you already know where you should be going. You already know what you should be doing and you already have what it takes to move forward. You may feel stuck and the only way to get unstuck is to move. So just move! Any kind of movement is good in helping you to get unstuck.

****
The first step is always the most difficult one because you are taking a step towards something that you are not familiar with
****

There are certain emotions, feelings, and thoughts that run through your mind and, at times, are just unbearable. Trust me; I know firsthand what that feels like. I have felt like that several times throughout my life and that feeling is absolutely heart-wrenching. I felt like I had no purpose in life. I would ask myself, "What on earth was I here for?" Since I grew up with a physical disability and limitations, I felt as if I would never do anything significant in life. Countless times I remember asking myself, "Will I ever do anything great in my life? What will I amount to? Will people respect me for who I am as a person?" I was always worrying about how other people would accept me and perceive me. All I ever wanted was to be normal and accepted, like everyone else. No more, no less just equal. Many people meet my disability before they meet me as a person. By that, I mean they judge the book by its cover and they judge me before even knowing anything about me.

To start, let me tell you a little bit about myself and how I was able to change my thought process to become successful. I was born with a rare neuromuscular disorder called Spinal Muscular Atrophy also known as S.M.A. It is one of the several Muscular Dystrophies that are out there. Due to a deficiency in the motor neuron cells, it makes my body weaker as I get older. It is one of the less progressive forms of the disease. It also limits me from doing certain basic daily activities like getting in and out of bed without assistance, lifting my arms above my head, getting dressed on my own, and even getting in and out of the shower by myself.

The specific cause of S.M.A is the lack of just one protein on the muscles that prevents them from maturing, growing, and functioning the way that they were created to function. It actually does the opposite and causes them to weaken at a slow pace. Can you believe that? The lack of just ONE protein causes me to have to live this "different" type of life. The good thing is that I don't experience much pain, just a little discomfort at times when my legs get cramped up or swollen from poor circulation and sitting in my wheelchair for 15-17 hours per day. I am fortunate enough to have a special wheelchair and bed that allows me to elevate my legs so that the circulation in my body can get the blood moving around.

The lack of just one protein is what causes me to live a different type of lifestyle than most people. I love to use the analogy of "THE POWER OF THE ONE". I use that analogy when speaking to people and I compare it with the ONE protein I'm missing that causes what I have. I do this because in life we are constantly making choices and decisions that affect our daily living. From really small and insignificant choices like what we want to eat for breakfast or what outfit we want to wear. To really big choices like what will I do today to get me closer to that

21

promotion at work or what can I do to reach my dreams and goals that can help me turn them into a reality?

In life, you can make just ONE choice or ONE decision that can cause you to live a different type of lifestyle. You can meet just ONE person that can help catapult you to the next level and take you places that you never dreamed would be possible. Or, you can make just ONE poor decision that can cost you everything (literally) and even cost you your life. I know many people who have been on the flip side of the coin and have made a poor decision that they are regretful for today. I also know some who aren't even here anymore to share about it.

Today I want to challenge you to ask yourself just one question; ***"What is that ONE choice or that ONE decision I am willing to make today that will impact my tomorrow?"*** One of my favorite authors John Maxwell said: *"Nothing ever happens in life until someone makes a decision. In fact, by not making a decision, a decision is already being made not to take action. Be someone who leads your life and not someone who simply accepts what happens. If you wait for life to happen to you, it will,* *however, it will not be the life you desire. To prevent this, we must learn to make good decisions and then manage those decisions. Successful people understand that you never go anywhere until you decide where it is you want to go."*

****

You can live an Indispensable life by embracing the amazing greatness that already lives inside of you today

****

Speaking as a person who is unable to walk, I know firsthand that many people take the smallest things for granted. Life is too short and that is why I made the decision to write this book. Regardless of your situation or your circumstance, I want you to know that you are still absolutely necessary and very important! There is a reason why you were given this life to live. This world needs you and that special thing that you have to offer. You possess special talents, skills, and gifts that no one is aware of and they can benefit from what you have to offer. But first, you have to conquer your fear and let it go without any reserve.

I have learned from personal experience that you cannot only dream of it but you have to go out there and actually do it! Grabbing hold of your dreams, chasing your dreams, or reaching your goals in life requires you to take some form of action. You have to do something. You have to take that leap of faith and give it a shot or you will never reach the place that you have always dreamed of.

Even writing your dreams and goals out on a piece of paper to make them visible, or by recording yourself with a cell phone, like I do, will motivate you to take that first step forward. You must listen to and visualize your goals every day. The point is to take the first step forward. The first step is always the most difficult one because you are taking a step towards something that you are not familiar with. The unknown is always a scary place to move towards but it is necessary if you ever plan on turning your dreams into a reality and arriving at the place that you have always envisioned.

Taking that first step means you are one step closer to living the life you deserve. You deserve to live the Indispensable life now! Even one small step forward is progress. Just because your progress isn't obvious doesn't mean your faith isn't working. Keep pressing forward! Some people think that's no big deal and yes you might not be where you want to be at this very moment but you are also not where you used to be either. You are doing more than what you did while you were sitting all cozy in your comfort zone not taking any steps at all and becoming stagnant. One of the world's top motivational speakers and my friend Les Brown is always saying, *"Shoot for the moon because even if you miss you will land among the stars."*

Nowadays, many people are not living their lives to the fullest because they haven't realized that they are Indispensable Now. Living life to the fullest and becoming Indispensable Now is not an easy thing to do, which is why most people aren't doing it. If it were easy to do, everyone would be doing it right? In order to live and become Indispensable Now you must be *willing to do the things today that other people don't do, in order to have the things tomorrow that other people won't have.* ~ *Les Brown*

One of the things you must be willing to do is dedicating yourself to a higher standard and everything

you do must lead towards excellence. Bring your A-game
to everything you do. Constantly raise the bar for
yourself. Whether it's on the job, at the gym, reaching
your goals, whatever it is, do it towards excellence. If you
learn to develop a habit of excellence and start doing the
very best you can, you will set yourself apart from
everyone else and the demand for what you have to offer
will increase.

The unknown will always try and stop you from
moving forward. It almost paralyzes you to the point
where you shrink back, but that is when you have to rise
up and go after it like never before! Remember don't just
dream it, DO IT! Be creative and step outside of the box.
You can't be INDISPENSABLE and IN THE BOX. You
can't be INDISPENSABLE and average at the same time.
You can't be INDISPENSABLE and mediocre, it will
never work. Being INDISPENSABLE NOW means that
you have to shift your thinking. Begin to think ridiculously
bigger than you ever have before. You have to act
differently, and do things in a different way.

People who are Indispensable are willing to be
creative and develop their ability to think outside of the

box. It can really set you apart when you are going through the problem-solving process. If you are able to think creatively and fix or help fix any problems that may arise, everyone will want you to be a part of their team. Remember, you can't be indispensable in the box. Challenge yourself to come up with new ways to do things. The end results will eventually pay off.

I remember when I felt it in my heart to start my own business. Not knowing how to start a business, or even run a business, I would say to myself, "You don't know what you are doing Jose. You don't have enough money, and you don't have any resources or connections." I was afraid to invest in myself for fear of failure. I shared with my wife Andrea the dream and the vision that I had about creating a company where people's lives would be impacted through my personal story of overcoming. I also wanted to create custom clothing; T-shirts that people could wear to become part of the family of Indispensables as well as a reminder to themselves that they too were Indispensable! After I told Andrea about the vision, she became my biggest advocate, my biggest supporter, and my biggest motivator. She was my personal cheerleader. She encouraged me like never before. She said things like,

27

"Honey we don't need to have a lot of money to get started; we just need to be willing and faithful that it will all work out." WOW! Now that is what I call positive thinking because our bank account was certainly saying something very different at the time.

She would also say things like, "Honey, you have a great life story and you are a great communicator. You need to share your story with others who feel or have felt the same way you did with everything that you have been through in life. You can be a big light in a dark world. You have a great personality and I think you have what it takes to be great!"

These were all the same thoughts that I already had but I just needed to hear it from someone else's mouth. I needed to hear those affirmations. I needed the reassurance to move forward in what I felt my purpose was in life and my wife was the one who gave me the push I needed to take the first step. Sometimes, all we need is a little push in order to take flight. If you do not have anyone in your life right now, let me be that push for you. As I mentioned before, the time is now! So spread your wings and fly as high as you can and enjoy the view!

While you're flying high, be willing to work hard and go the extra mile. People who are indispensable usually expand their role by going above and beyond the scope of their responsibilities. You might be saying things today like, "I don't have time for this. I don't get paid for that part of my job, or this is not in my job description". Whatever the job is, make it a point of helping others succeed and maximizing their potential.

All great and successful leaders continually make sure that their people are always learning and growing. The problem is that many people believe that by helping others they are hurting themselves when in fact the opposite is true. Zig Ziglar said, *"You can have everything in life that you want, if you will just help enough other people get what they want."* People get excited when they feel that you have exceeded their expectation of you. I've heard it said that it is always better to under promise and over deliver. In the business world, successful companies keep their customers happy by giving them more than what they think they paid for. If you can make people feel like they are getting more than what they paid for, then you have just gained yourself a loyal customer.

You will also need to be willing to learn to express your appreciation for others and lift them up, regardless of what's going on around you. I know we live in a busy world and it's tough to pause to recognize someone else's work when we are engrossed in our own work. But if you can purpose to take some time out to appreciate and honor those you work with, it can make all the difference in the world. It will also make them want to be around you. Everyone enjoys being appreciated. It can also make them want to go the extra mile for you as well.

I have always had an encouraging spirit but I never knew that my voice would be the very thing that I would use as an adult to get this message of hope out to the world. To spread this message of hope everywhere I go and to everyone I meet. It's funny how at times, the things you know you are good at could be the very things that you are also afraid of. Notice how I used the word things, plural because you can have multiple gifts and talents. You are not restricted to only having one good thing about you. I was losing my ability to do a lot of things physically but I thank God I never lost my voice, my personality, or my sense of humor. I realized that the same thing that was

30

making my body weaker on the outside was the same thing that was making me stronger on the inside.

****

Remember don't just dream it, DO IT

****

Now I am proud to say that I speak all over the world encouraging and motivating thousands of people at conferences, business seminars, large and small corporations, universities, and nonprofits every year. Some of the topics I speak about are on being Indispensable Now and not letting your struggles become your standard even when the odds may look like they are stacked against you. I have seen so many people go through life because of whatever their situation or circumstance is, be it physical or mental and just feel unwanted, unimportant, and undervalued. This is why I started doing what I do because there is a need in this world for people to feel wanted and needed. Everyone has something of value to offer and to bring to the table. Everybody needs to know that there are people out there that need what you have to offer!

Learning to appreciate that life is about connection and sharing our stories is another aspect you must also be willing to do. As you share your story, we learn that as human beings, we all want love, peace, and happiness in our lives. I enjoy hearing other people's stories and sharing mine as well. Being able to share your story, especially with someone who is going through what you have already gone through, helps to bring healing and encouragement to the situation. And it doesn't always have to be a similar situation. I love when I am able to share my story of living life in a wheelchair with an individual or group of people because it just gives them hope to be able to get through whatever situation or circumstance that they may be going through at the moment. No one likes being alone for a long time. People love sharing life together. That's how long lasting relationships are developed, through connecting our stories. People who are living life to the fullest and being Indispensable are focused on making a real difference in the lives of others. Climbing to the top of a mountain can be lonely if you are there all by yourself, so why not bring some people with you and have a party. Always stay positive. Being indispensable doesn't come from ego but from what others think of you as you help them

HOW TO BE INDISPENSABLE

succeed and flourish. It doesn't mean you puff your chest out like you're the king of the jungle. It means that you are willing to be brave enough to make sure that you help others stay on the path to success. If people are comfortable being around you, then they will be comfortable being there for you and not against you.

I want you to know that you have what it takes, right now, to get started. Do not let another moment go by. I want you to place your hand over your heart right now. Do you feel that beating? That's what's called purpose my friends. For as long as your heart is beating, there is purpose, gifts, and talents within you, right now, which you can tap into and bring your dreams to reality. Now that you know you have everything inside of you this very moment, go ahead take the first step! I dare you to see what happens!

****
"What is the ONE choice or ONE decision I am willing to make today, that will impact my tomorrow?"
****

Action Steps

Live and Become Indispensable Now

o *Dedicate yourself to high standards and try to do everything you do towards excellence. Bring your best and bring your A-game to everything you do. Constantly raise the bar for yourself.*

o *Work hard and go the extra mile. People who are indispensable usually expand their role by going beyond their scope and their responsibilities. Whatever their job is, they make it a point of helping others succeed and maximize their potential.*

o *Be a part of the plan and solution; not the problem.*

o *Learn to be creative and develop your ability to think outside of the box.*

o *Learn to express your appreciation for others and lift them up, regardless of what's going on around you.*

o *Learn to appreciate that life is about connection and sharing our stories. As you share your stories, you learn that as human beings, we all want love, peace, and happiness in our lives.*

o *Always stay positive. Being indispensable doesn't come from ego but from what others think of you as you help them succeed and flourish.*

o *People who are Indispensable are focused on making a real difference in the lives of others.*

Scan the QR code below for a special video about being Indispensable

CHAPTER 2

Recognize and Realize Your Uniqueness

When I was younger I never really paid much attention to the things I was good at doing because I was more focused on what I couldn't do. When you focus more on the negative, the positive shrinks, but when you focus more on the positive then the negative shrinks. The question I want to ask you today is; what are you shrinking in your life? Are you more focused on what you cannot do? Or are you more focused on what you can do? Before you can even begin to live this Indispensable life, you have to start thinking positively. All that stinking thinking must be thrown away. Some of the hardest times people go through in life are very visible. You can actually see them going through it and recognize when they are going through a difficult time. But then there are other things that people go through that are invisible and you cannot see what's going on because it's internal. So how do you know if a person is or isn't persevering through a struggle that you cannot see? The answer is; you cannot. That's why it's so important to share your personal stories with other people of what you've been through, how you overcame it, or what you may currently be going through and how you are overcoming it now!

The reality is that unless the hard times you go through are visible, no one will ever know what you are going through unless you tell them. So don't ever be afraid, shy, or embarrassed to share your story because there is power in your story and an even greater power in sharing it. It is important to recognize and realize that every time you share your story, you release that power, and you empower others to overcome as well. I've learned that sharing your story is an amazing experience because you never know who's listening to you or who's watching you and who can be encouraged or transformed by how you got through the storm.

From this moment on, I want you to start telling yourself every day, and every chance you get, that YOU ARE A WINNER. Say affirmations like, "I AM ABSOLUTELY NECESSARY, I WILL BE SUCCESSFUL in life, and MY DREAMS WILL COME TRUE." I have come across many guys in sales that were once very successful but for some reason or another got, what I like to call "stuck in their head". We often know exactly what to do to reach our goals and succeed but we get stuck in our own heads by focusing on the negative. We start focusing on all the things we can't do. You begin to tell yourself so many negative things that you start to believe them. As a result, you get "stuck". Well, today you are getting unstuck! Today is the day that you look in the mirror and conquer the person in the mirror by saying, you will be great, and you will accomplish your goals your dreams.

****
The more effective you are the more sought after you become
****

I was motivated to write this book when I started realizing that I am in control of the choices and decisions that I make. I wanted to share these things with the world and perhaps help someone else realize what; they too, are good at doing. I want to help people learn how to utilize what they have and what they can do to make a difference in their own sphere of influence. Other than speaking, I am a corporate trainer and CEO. I am very good at motivating and encouraging people to learn more, do more, and become more in life; so that they can get the most out of life that they possibly can. There's greatness in everyone, there is greatness in you and trust me, there is enough greatness inside of everyone for everyone to be great!

I like to say that you do not recognize that you are indispensable until you realize that you are different. You see most people think that recognizing and realizing mean the same thing, but they don't. *Recognizing* means that you *identify with something or someone from having encountered them before* and so you recognize it because it's familiar to you. You recognize when you are using your gift or talent because it's built inside of you. You were born with it. It is part of your DNA and you are good at it, so you recognize it. You recognize when you do it because you've done it before. Remember it's already inside of you, so all you need to do is master it and become an expert at it. Your gift will make room for you if you will make room for it and start to develop it.

It's like being an artist. You may be good at drawing or painting and you know this to be true because after you look at your work you say, "Wow, this came out great! I'm good at this!" Being artistic doesn't come easy to everyone, but if it does for you, then it's part of your greatness! The cool thing about recognizing your gift is that once you do, you can use it to become massively successful in life. Have you ever noticed that people will pay for experts? Once you become an expert in your gifted area, people will want what you have to offer and your demand will skyrocket. The more effective you are the more sought after you will become. Now all you need to do is turn it from being good, to being great and the doors will begin to open for you!

I was at a speaker-training event in Orlando, Florida at the Gaylord Palms Convention Center. I was sharing my story with a group of people on how my wife and my children have to help me get dressed and out of the bed every morning. I also shared how they need to physically lift me up and put me into my wheelchair every day, just so I can live somewhat of a normal life. I told them that after my wife or one of my children helps me get into my wheelchair, it's up to me to lift myself up mentally. I have to prepare myself to be in my wheelchair for 15 to 17 hours each day. It's up to me to prepare myself mentally to succeed and win.

When I was done sharing my story, the audience was asked if they had any comments or feedback they wanted to share. A young guy by the name of Demo stood up and said, "You know what Jose? I am usually not one to ever be at a loss for words but I don't even know what to say right now. I don't think that I will ever forget what you just said about getting up in the morning and the process that you have to go through every day just to get dressed and out of bed. I don't think that anyone in this room ever thinks twice about getting out of their bed in the morning, getting dressed and furthermore, needing someone to help them on a daily basis." He said, "I think that whenever I wake up in the morning from now on and I don't feel like getting up, I am going to be thinking about what you have to go through every day, wow!" He had this look on his face that you just knew he could never imagine having to go through what I have to go through.

My story made Demo *realize* that there are some things in life that some people can't do, that other people take for granted. His life was transformed and impacted that day, forever. I was grateful for him sharing the feedback. I did not know until afterward that this guy "Demo", who my story impacted, is a Latin Grammy Award-winning producer whose real name is Demacio Castellon. He has produced/engineered/collaborated with some of the greatest artists in the world such as Madonna, Jay Z, Michael Jackson, Lady Gaga, and Justin Timberlake just to name a few. I also found out that he was married to the famous Grammy award winning singer and songwriter Nelly Furtado.

You see he was an expert in his field. A world-renowned Grammy winner yet my story impacted him. I am able to share my story to thousands of people because although my struggle is still very real and I have not "fully overcome" my struggles, like many of you have. I have realized that I do have a gift. My gift is my voice and I have become an expert at telling my story to bring transformation into people's lives.

Realizing means *you become fully aware of something as a fact*, and the *fact* is, you are Indispensable Now because you are different. That's right! I said it! You are different! You have to realize that you were created uniquely. There is no one else on this planet that is exactly like you. Even identical twins aren't exactly alike. Some people have the same similarities as you, but there is no one else *exactly* like you. No one has the same mojo that you possess. You are one of a kind, an original, and genuinely made! If you never recognize what it is that makes you Indispensable, you will never become fully aware of the fact that you are and you will continue to live the mediocre life. You were never created to be ordinary; you were created to be extraordinary!

Most people do not think the exact way that you do. They do not have the exact views or creativity that you have, and they definitely do not dream like you do! *I know you're a big dreamer!* You're probably thinking about your dream right now and I hope that you are motivated to move towards it. Sometimes in life, we forget who we are and we don't even recognize who we have become.

****
You do not recognize that you are Indispensable
until you realize that you are different
****

Start realizing who you were created to be, who you always wanted to be, and the type of life that you always wanted to live. Watch and see what happens in your life when you start recognizing yourself again. It's ok to be different because being different is also very attractive. Remember you recognize that you are Indispensable when you realize that you are different.

For example, I was at church and this lady came up to me whom I had never seen before. She said, "You know what? There is something very different about you. You have a great smile and you are such an inspiration to so many without even knowing it. Don't you ever lose that smile; it's like a ray of sunshine that just brightens up the room." I was so honored and taken back that she had the courage and the boldness to even share that with me because most people don't. That's the beauty of living your life to the fullest. People will recognize your uniqueness because it just shines all over you. You do not have to brag about it because everybody will see it. People will be able to see your joy and your character by the way you act and live your life, regardless of what you are going through.

Have you ever noticed that when exotic cars drive by that everybody turns their head to look at them? They are not only looking at it because it's exotic and beautiful but because it's different and unique and not something that they see every day. I will use myself as an example. Every time I go into a room, or do a speaking engagement or an event, or even at restaurants and in public areas, people are always staring at me. I would like to think that they are staring at me because I am somewhat handsome, and even though my wife may agree with me, the reality is that they are staring at me because I look different and unique. I'm not the type of person that they usually see every day or on a normal basis. You don't usually see people in wheelchairs riding around everywhere like I do with a big smile on their face. By nature, people are attracted to the things that don't look normal, average, mediocre or status quo. People are drawn to uniqueness and attractiveness.

Look at Stevie Wonder, Ray Charles, and Andrea Bocelli for example. They are all highly gifted in the art of music. People are attracted to them not only because they are very talented men who know music, but also because they are different from many other musicians. They all pushed passed their limitation of being blind musicians and became very successful at it. They recognized and realized their gifts and became experts in their genre. Fans pay to see them in person.

I want to encourage you right now and tell you this; don't be like the rest of them; be one of the best of them. Be the best in whatever you desire. Master it and then get paid for it! Never give up on your dreams, never settle for less, and never stop believing in yourself. It is your dream and you own it! It belongs to you and no one else, so now it's time to wake up and go get it! Make it fun, make it exciting, and make it your reality! Since you are reading this book I want you to recognize and realize the fact that you are unique, you are different, and you are attractive, so go start making those heads turn everywhere you go!

****

Don't be like the rest of them; be one of the best of them

****

Before I move on to the next chapter, I would also like to let you know since I'm talking about recognizing and realizing your gifts, talents, and your dreams, that you cannot share your dreams with everyone *at first*. There are dream killers out there who will try to kill your dreams before they even become a reality (yes even friends and family). Since a lot of people are scared and afraid to fulfill their own dreams, they do not want you fulfilling yours. Be very careful with whom you share your dreams with because not everyone is in your corner and not everyone is cheering for you. Some people want you to fail and some are hoping you will. I believe you won't!

Action Steps

How to Recognize and Realize What Your Gifts and Talents Are

- ➤ *What are you passionate about?*

- ➤ *What is it that makes you attractive?*

- ➤ *What special skills do you have that can set you apart?*

- ➤ *What are you really good at doing and what do you love to do?*

- ➤ *What is it about YOU that makes you different or unique?*

Scan the QR code below for a special video on recognizing and realizing your uniqueness

CHAPTER 3
Believing In The Impossible!

In order to believe in the impossible, you must first believe in yourself so that you may achieve the impossible. If you can conceive it and receive it, then you can achieve it. Be yourself and don't be ashamed of who you are because everyone loves those who love being themselves. When you believe in yourself, you will be on your way to successful living. What we learn, what we earn, and what we believe is a direct result of what we believe about ourselves. If you believe that you will only make $15 per hour working at a job then you will only make $15 per hour. However, if you believe you that you can make $500 dollars per hour then you are going to figure out ways to make that happen.

"What we can or cannot do, what we consider possible or impossible, is rarely a function of our true capability. It is more likely a function of our beliefs about who we are." –
Anthony Robbins

The most important objective to achieve anything on this planet (or out of this world) is to believe in it. Without belief, there is nothing. Have you ever thought about doing something but thought it was so huge that you never thought you would be capable of doing it? You know what I'm talking about. That one dream or that one goal you have always had that was so huge that you knew it could only happen in a dream. The dream that you always thought was impossible and could never become a reality or never come true. Well, I want you to take a quick moment right now (seriously!) Lay the book down, close your eyes, and think about the one thing in your life that you have desired to come true. A dream that is so big that it just seems impossible. Okay, do it now. Close your eyes and visualize that dream. Visualize that place you want to go to. When you are done, come back to me. I'll be waiting right here.

Did you do it? If you didn't, stop right now and visualize in your mind your dream or that specific goal you desire. Can you see your dream? Now I want you to do something that you might think is a little crazy, but I have learned that looking a little crazy sometimes can produce a big buzz and big results. I want you to tell yourself and say it out loud right now. Do not worry about who is around you, do not worry about who is looking at you. If you are serious about attaining what you just visualized and believe that it's impossible, I want you to say with conviction and with everything that is inside of you; ALL THINGS ARE POSSIBLE TO THOSE WHO BELIEVE and today I AM A BELIEVER!

How did that feel? Did you say it with conviction? Did you actually believe it? If not then do it again. You see the word impossible actually spells IM-POSSIBLE, which means it is possible for you to do it! From this point forward I want you to start thinking about and believing in what you cannot see, because if you do, eventually you will begin to see what you have been believing in.

****

What we learn, what we earn, and what we believe is a direct result of what we believe of ourselves

****

As long as you believe long enough and work hard enough there is no other choice but for it to show up in your life. There are so many people who live their lives just getting by, accepting, and settling at the place where they are, even though they do not want to be there. This happens because they have stopped believing, they have stopped dreaming, and hope is no longer alive.

****

The moment you stop believing in the thing that you thought was impossible; you experience the flat line syndrome

****

The impossible just seems so far off and so distant that they don't even want to think about it. Their vision of it becomes blurry. Like a thick fog that they cannot see through. They conform to their situation or circumstance with the mindset that there is nothing else out there for them. They think they will never be able to achieve any more in life than what they currently have and that this is the life they have to live and so they settle for it. If you are thinking that, I am here to tell you that settling is a lie that you have been telling yourself. Get rid of that thought. It's time to switch it up now and start telling yourself positive things and start believing in what you are saying.

Let us try it again. Now this time I really want you to place the book down and say, ALL THINGS ARE POSSIBLE TO THOSE WHO BELIEVE and today I AM A BELIEVER! The key is this; believe in what you cannot see at this current moment and know that it is on its way. You have to believe it before you will ever see it! There will always be distractions in life that try to throw you off track, but you just keep going. Never stop, never give up, and never give in!

I am pretty sure you have heard the saying "keep hope alive." You want to know why they say that, because the moment you stop hoping or believing in the thing that you thought was impossible, is the moment that you experience what I like to call the *flat line syndrome*. That's right, everything just dies out because you have pulled the plug on your own life support, and your dream or vision becomes flat lined. That is why it is so critical to stay away from the flat line syndrome mentality because it is literally a matter of life or death. The question is not whether or not what you dream of doing is actually possible. The real question is do you *believe* it is possible? If you believe it then you can do it. If you can see it; you can say it (speak it out loud and speak life into the atmosphere) and if you can hold on to it for long enough then you can have it.

If you would have told me 10 years ago that I would be speaking on the same stage as my mentor and friend, Les Brown, I would have never believed it or even thought it would be possible. If you would have told me 10 years ago that I would be speaking to thousands of people, students, and organizations, impacting them to know they are valuable and Indispensable Now, I would have never believed it. If you would have told me that I would become an author and write books I would have thought you were crazy and out of your mind. If you would have told me that I would be training corporations on how to develop Indispensable employees, I would have looked you square in the eyes and said, you're crazy! I've been passed up for promotions plenty of times because of this wheelchair. Yet all of these things have become possible because I made a decision to start believing in the impossible.

****

There will always be distractions in life that try to throw you off track, but you just keep going. Never stop, never give up, and never give in!

****

I decided to start believing outrageously, to start believing like it's going to happen today and now, and started believing like never before.

"So many of our dreams at first seem impossible, then they seem improbable, and then, when we summon the will, they soon become inevitable."

– Christopher Reeve

You have nothing to lose and everything to gain so go ahead, take the leap of faith, jump and be amazing in everything you do. Keep on dreaming, keep on envisioning, and keep on believing in the impossible. When you do, your life will be transformed and changed forever and the people who are depending on you will be glad you did and so will you.

The formula is simple: Believe and then Become! You may be asking, is that it? Yep, and you better believe it! Start to ask yourself, *what do I want?* Do I really want to continue working this 9-5 job for someone else and making their dreams come true, when I know I have what it takes to reach my own dreams? Now I'm not saying to go and quit your job tomorrow. You need that income to fund your dream. However, as you work on your dream part-time, it will eventually become your full-time passion. Notice that I did not say full-time *job*. When you do what you love to do, you will never work a day in your life. It no longer becomes a burden or a headache. Instead, it gives you a happy and joyful life. You wake up every day with a new passion and pep in your step because you are doing what you love to do. If you are willing to put in the work, it will take you further than you could have ever imaged.

****
The formula is simple:
Believe and then Become!
****

Maybe you are already self-employed or work in sales. Ask yourself, am I really satisfied with where I am now? Was this the company, and the income that I sought after when I was bringing forth my dream? Truth is, many of us will say no. There will always be something bigger and better that we can aim to accomplish if we believe we can do it. A good friend of mine was a successful realtor for many years. She had dreams of becoming a broker and offering specialized services when she first started. Well, after several years in the business, the money was good but truth be told, there was really no passion. Although she was, in essence living a great life, she was not really living her dream. She was only living a fraction of that dream. Yet as she began to believe in herself, she realized that the services she wanted to provide were *Indispensable Now* in the industry! So she embarked on becoming a real-estate broker and she created a brokerage that offers concierge home buying and rental services.

She caters to the wealthy and elite and provides them with concierge services from buying luxury homes, luxury rental homes, and even tickets to different shows and events while they may be visiting from out of town and are house hunting. Her offices are now located in a prime waterfront location. All this was possible because she was no longer satisfied with experiencing the flat line syndrome and living a fraction of her dreams! Ask yourself this question; am I satisfied with living a fraction of my dream? Or am I willing to step out in faith and work harder and smarter to bring my dream, my *true* dream, into reality?

It has been said that 85 percent of Americans in the United States are going to a job that they hate. Maybe you desired to become a teacher, a doctor, or any other service oriented field. Ask yourself, am I doing for others what I dreamed of when I first started following my dreams? Many times, especially in the service-oriented field, it's a thankless job. As a result, we can become like robots just doing what we know how to do through the education that we have obtained (doing the same ole, same ole). You dreamed of becoming a teacher to make a difference in the lives of the students. Yet, you complain every day going to work and you are miserable.

As an entry-level teacher, the pay is not that great in some states but that is not the reason you wanted to become a teacher. You dreamed of becoming a teacher to transform the lives of the students in your school. What happened to that passion? What happened to that burning desire to make a difference and see the change you wanted to bring? Don't let anything stop you from reaching your destiny! If you believe that you are Indispensable, how awesome would it be for your students to feel and know that they are too? Teachers are the dream lifters for many students. Teachers have the ability to inspire and motivate kids like no one else can. Some teachers, the ones that have gone above and beyond are a big part of who we have become today!

Maybe you wanted to become a doctor to save lives, yet you push medications instead of taking extra time to care for the whole person. Or maybe you actually do love going to work but it has become just that, WORK. Ask yourself, why did you start this journey in the first place? What is missing from your dream? What has yet to be fulfilled? Let me say this, if you focus solely on the money instead of your mission, you will never be satisfied. This applies to having an abundance of money or having a little. There will always be something missing; money will never fill that void.

****

There has to be something deep inside that moves you and most often that extra push comes from a desire to truly help others

****

I was speaking at an event and a young woman approached me. She said that she was working towards becoming a neurosurgeon but was thinking about quitting because she really did not know if she could do it. After she heard me speak and I shared my story with her, she came up to me at the end and said that she realized now that she was meant to become a neurosurgeon. My story reminded her of *why* she sought after her dream to become a neurosurgeon in the first place. It was to help others like me and to help find a cure for neurological diseases like the one I have S.M.A.

Just doing something that you desire is not enough. She could do it, she had what it took to become a neurosurgeon but unless your dreams add value to the lives of others, you will be unsatisfied and may even give up on your dreams. There has to be something deep inside that moves you and most often that extra push comes from a desire to truly help others. Who knows, this young woman may be the very person who finds a cure for my disease that allows me to walk again and leave my wheelchair behind. All things are possible if we believe!

Now my next question to you is; do you really believe you can do it? We all know people who talk about their big dreams, who claim to be "making things happen" but when you look at them, they are going nowhere. Most of the time, they are spending a bunch of money to *"make"* something happen. However, the real issue is that they do not actually believe in themselves. You can spend the money to go to college. You can spend the money to open a business. You can even spend the money to open the charity you have always dreamed of, BUT do you really believe that you can do it?

There are going to be times when you are chasing your dreams and you feel like you want to give up, and times when nothing seems to be happening. There will be times when the doors of opportunity seemed to be closed. In fact, some of those doors are definitely closed. You have tried everything but you keep hitting a dead end. It is in moments like these when you have to ask yourself, do I believe in ME? If you believe in yourself, if you can see and visualize the dream, then there is nothing that can stop you. You may have setbacks, sure, but Indispensables are people who believe in themselves when no one else does.

Do you know how many times I was told I would never have a "normal" life because of my disability? Look around, there are not many people in wheelchairs that own a home, drive their own cars, own and operate a business, and travel all over the world. The few that do are part of the family of Indispensables. They do not let anything stop them from living life to the fullest. If you are living your dreams, then you too are part of the family of Indispensables! I know that many of you right now have had your dreams shot down by family members, friends, and people you care about that told you that you are crazy for thinking you can do the impossible. Guess what? I believe in you. Again I ask you, do you believe in yourself? If you answered yes, then what is stopping you? I hope that after you have read this chapter, your answer will also be that nothing is going to stop you. If that is true, then welcome to the family of Indispensables!

Now that you know what you want and you believe in yourself, *what is the first step you're going to take to get one step closer to achieve what you have been longing for?* If you have ever been to an Olympic style pool with diving boards, you see brave young kids climbing up the diving steps and definitely excited to get to the top. One step at a time, they are carefully climbing. When they finally arrive, you can see the horrified look on their faces. They pause, walk slowly to the edge, glance at the pool and make a decision. Everyone around is yelling, "Jump, Jump, Jump!" They either decide to jump or they decide to climb back down. Two things happen, either they jump and realize it was not that big of a deal and do it again because it was fun and they knew they could do it. Or they climb back down and always wonder what would have happened if they jumped. Taking the first step with any decision is always the hardest. I say go ahead and jump!

However, through this journey of life, we will always be taking "first steps" with something new. New things come into our lives, new opportunities, and new people; there will always be the first step. The key is determining what that first step will be. Like the child at the pool, the first step was climbing the ladder to get to the diving board. He already made the decision that he wanted to jump, so his first step was getting to the top. After he was there, he had to make another decision; to actually jump or retreat. Sometimes on your ladder of success, there will be opportunities to jump and opportunities to retreat. Nevertheless, if you do not make a decision to climb for what you want, you will never reach the level of success you desire. If you have made a decision and then later decide that you need to reevaluate your plan that is perfectly okay. Determine another way to make it happen or change the direction entirely. That choice will be up to you. However, you will have to accept responsibility for the decisions you make. Remember that just because it is a good step, does not necessarily mean that it is the right step for the season you are in. You never want to be that person who wonders, "What would have happened if I did it?"

Since you have carefully thought out your first step, now it is time to ask yourself, w*hat is my plan to get from Point A to Point B?* Count the cost of each step and do not despise small beginnings. Hewlett-Packard is a billion-dollar company that started in the 1930's with $538.00 in a garage. Bill Hewlett and David Packard grew the company into one of the world's largest information technology companies. When they started in their garage in the 1930's, technology and electronics were not even as advanced as they are now. I'm sure there were many people who said they were wasting their time, they will never make any money in electronics and technology. Now 77 years later HP has more than 300,000 employees and posted revenues at one time over $126 billion. It all started because they knew what they wanted, they believed in themselves, they took the first step to open the company and continued to plan and execute. They did not know all the answers. They could not connect all the dots from point A to Z, but they could surely start planning from point A to B! They made what seemed impossible, possible because they believed in themselves. You can too! Start your plan today.

Maybe you want to lose weight and nothing seems to be working. Sometimes it can feel impossible and so overwhelming trying to get everything right. The good news is you don't have to know everything. You just have to start. Start small and plan ahead. They say if you fail to plan then you plan to fail. Don't worry about where you are a month from now. Take it week-by-week or day-by-day. Regardless of the struggle, you do not have to let it become your standard. Do you really want it? Do you really believe that you can do it? What is the first step you will take and how will you get to the next step daily? My friends, better yet, my family of Indispensables, I want you to know that I believe in you and I know you can live the indispensable life you have always dreamed of.

Action Steps

Start Believing For The Impossible

➢ *Ask yourself what is it that you think is impossible that you want out of life?*

➢ *Create a plan to get from Point A to Point B and so on.*

➢ *Take the first step towards getting closer to what you have been longing for.*

➢ *Believe it, see it, receive it, and achieve it!*

Scan the QR code below for a special video on believing in the impossible

CHAPTER 4
Purpose and Potential

"The greatest good you can do for another is not just share your riches, but reveal to them their own." ~ Disraeli

The word purpose by definition is the reason for which something is done, created, or for which something exists. Many people ask themselves that question all the time. Why do I exist or what was I created for? What is my purpose in life? Most of the time when people ask themselves this question, it is because they do not feel important and they are trying to find their importance in life.

You may be asking yourself, how do I know if I am living my true life purpose? Here is an easy way to find out. If you are not waking up every morning filled with excitement, energy, and passion, then chances are; you're probably not living your true-life purpose. We live in a world where we are told more about our limitations than we are about our potential. Purpose is not something that you gain, acquire, or have to work to get. It is important to understand that everyone is *born* with a purpose already inside of him or her. When you find your meaning, what your purpose is, you will work harder to reach your goals and to better yourself and those around you.

****

If you do not use your God-given gifts, talents, and abilities then you are cheating yourself and others out of the life that was intended for you and them

****

I have heard it said that the purpose of life is to discover your gift. The work of life is to develop it and the meaning of life is to give it away. We are bombarded by doubts and fears that many times keep us from living out the purposes that have been established for us. There is much more meaning to life once you realize your purpose for living. When you live your life not knowing your

72

purpose, you live with a sense of emptiness or lack of fulfillment. I am sure many of us can relate. Whether you are reading this and don't know what your purpose is or you're excelling in your purpose, at one time there was a moment when we did not know what our purpose was or how to bring it to fruition.

I remember having a conversation with myself and asking, what do I want to do with my life? I knew there was more to life than just sitting and dying in this wheelchair. I wanted something different and I wanted it bad. I just did not know how to go after it. To be honest with you, I was afraid of it. I didn't know if there was anything out there for me. The unknown is always a scary and fearful place to have to encounter (and we will talk about that in the next chapter) but it can also be a very good place. I knew I had the gift of speaking, inspiring, and motivating others but it was on a small scale and I wanted to do it big. Real big!

That is why it is so important to live a purpose driven life and to know that you were created for something greater than just merely existing. You were created with special gifts and abilities to be used in a good

73

and positive way. Your purpose for living is not only for you but also for the benefit of others around you. You were created to impact, inspire, and influence people's lives. If you do not use your God-given gifts, talents, and abilities then you are cheating yourself and others out of the life that was intended for you and them. Remember your purpose was not given for you alone, but for the benefit of others as well.

Speaking was my purpose and it was my gift. It was the very thing I was supposed to be doing all along. I knew I could do it but I was scared of doing it on a much larger scale. One thing that I am so grateful for is that while my arms, legs, and body were getting weaker and weaker, my voice and my confidence were getting stronger and stronger.

****

Turn your struggle into strength

****

I began to use my voice more effectively and thanking God for using me to be a vessel of impact. Did I know where I was going or where this path was going to

HOW TO BE INDISPENSABLE

take me? No, I did not. Did I know that I would meet my mentor Les Brown and become his protégé in less than a year? No, I did not. Yet, I stepped out in faith and began the journey of becoming a professional motivational and transformational speaker and trainer.

They say that the best ideas and inventions are all located in the cemetery. Why? Countless people have taken their dreams to the grave with them. Have you ever thought of an idea but never did anything with it? Then years later you see someone else who thought of the same idea, except they acted on it and now they are living the Indispensable life.

There is something inside of us that exuberates joy when we are living our dreams. It doesn't matter the cost because we receive so much joy from it. Yet, when we see other people performing on the idea that was ours, all we can do is shake our head in disappointment. Or is it? Do you think that you were just given one idea? Of course not! You were given multiple gifts, ideas, talents, and creativity. If you do not act on one of them, then look for another. It's time to stop wasting time.

You may be reading this book and thinking, "Okay Jose, I get what you're saying but I have no clue how to find my passion?" Or, maybe you're thinking that you were not born with any creative ideas or skills. Or just maybe, you know you have a gift but you do not know if that is truly what you should be doing. Regardless of whether you know what your purpose is or not, the good news is that you can find out what your purpose is and you can be successful in it!

I want to ask you some questions. Really take some time and think about your answers. What is it that makes you come alive? What is it that you wake up every morning wishing you could be doing? What is it that you could be doing, that you love so much, you would do it for free because you are just so passionate about it? We all have that feeling on the inside of us when something makes us really happy or excited. We also have that inner urge to make a difference in a certain area or want to see a change in something that makes us sad or uneasy until we figure out a way to change it. It is there that you will find your purpose.

****

You will only reach the level of success that you are willing to work for

****

I was at an event a few years back and ran into a couple that had sold everything here in the Unites States and was traveling to establish residence in Amsterdam. They were headed to Amsterdam to start a safe house in the red light district. The Red Light District is actually a legal tourist attraction where young women flaunt themselves, in very little clothing, in storefront windows like a piece of clothing for sale. Many times these ladies are forced to work. Their passports have been taken and they have no resources to leave. She and her husband were devastated by all the stories they were hearing about sexual abuse and sex trafficking. Deeply troubled by the injustice they were determined to do something about it. You may be asking yourself, "Why on earth would a couple leave the Unites States, travel to a foreign country, in the worst part of town, and possibly put themselves in danger to help these women? Simply put: *Passion*!

Their hearts were breaking for these women and they could not shake the feeling. Every night the young

77

wife explained that she would go to the district and befriend the young women on display in the windows. Without revealing too much of what they did, to protect their safety, they were able to save several women from this horrible lifestyle. These women escaped the district and now live normal lives because of the passion of just one couple. Just one couple who followed their hearts and made a difference in not only these women's lives but their future generations as well. What injustice is burning inside of you? What moves you? Finding passion isn't always birthed from happy moments. Like this couple, some find their purpose when they are deeply troubled to make a change!

Others determine their purpose when finding their strengths and weaknesses. After you know what you are good at, then you can focus on developing your strengths. Many people spend too much time focusing on strengthening their weaknesses instead of growing their strengths. Trying to get better at what you are weak at doing is not a bad thing, but you should be spending as much time as possible maximizing your strengths. However, I will also show you in a later chapter how to turn your weaknesses into WINS!

When I was young I had no idea what my purpose was and I didn't know what on earth I was here for or what I was supposed to do in life. I mean I had dreams, ambitions, and aspirations like everyone else does but that was all they were, only dreams. I actually thought that because I had a disability that I was not capable of doing anything great in life. I thought I was going to be like the average Joe, living an average Joe life, and just doing average things. That thought would pain me. It would literally hurt my heart to think, this is how my life is going to be because of this wheelchair.

****
Turn your purpose into passion, your passion into profit, and your profit into helping people
****

It took me a long while to figure it out. Like many others, it wasn't until I was well into my adulthood that I realized what the purpose for my life really was. I remember when I did my first speaking engagement. The responses and their reactions to what I said were amazing. Afterward, people would tell me that my story of overcoming adversity had encouraged them to want to be more and achieve more in life. At that very moment, I

79

figured out that I could use my gift of speaking to inspire and help transform other people's ways of thinking and in reality their lives! That was when I realized what my purpose was and I started working hard on maximizing my full potential. I also began to realize that the wheelchair and many of my struggles were all part of my purpose.

Now I am able to turn those struggles into stories to help motivate people to understand and see that they do not have to let their struggle become their standard any longer. You may be going through a difficult time right now and struggling tremendously so I want to tell you this, turn your struggle into strength. You never know, it just may be part of your purpose and your story too. I understand that overcoming any struggle takes work. However, you will only reach the level of success that you are willing to work for. Success takes work!

****

Greatness, Power, and Impact do not live in comfort zones

****

That is why I'm so passionate about what I do and that is why I am doing everything I can, (even writing this book) to help as many people as I can to realize what their purpose and passion are for their lives. I want to help people maximize their human potential. When you finally realize what your purpose is in life and why God created you, you get a new sense of living. It's like you're catapulted to another level of life to experience. Your whole life will change and the transformational journey will begin.

Your passion is now pursued; your impact is communicated, and then expands into the lives of so many others. The way you begin to look at things now will completely change in your thought process. What once was a thought has now become real life.

The dream does not stop once you have accomplished it. Let new dreams and bigger aspirations fuel you. Your outlook on life and what you thought it was supposed to be like is now altered because you have been exposed to another level; a new dimension of thinking, which now requires a new game plan and a new strategy.

If you are looking at your struggles, and telling yourself that you will never amount to anything great, you won't. If you look at your dream, which I am hoping is far bigger then what you can image, and you say that you are never going to accomplish it, you won't. Make sure that your thought process is positive. Be positive about accomplishing your dreams but also understand that it takes time. Don't be too hard on yourself; take it one day at a time. Grind every day to make your dream become a reality. Turn your purpose into passion, your passion into profit, and your profit into helping people. The 4 P's to living the Indispensable Life (Purpose, Passion, Profit, and People). Use the purpose you have now (what you are good at) and develop the passion for it. Do not ignore the passion. Don't allow others to down play your passion. Then, let your passion bring you profits. After you have become a master at your purpose, you will become passionate about it, and now that you are making a profit from it, teach other people how to do the same! It all comes full circle and it starts with YOU!

Sometimes life can feel like a game but remember you are playing to win. Having a mindset that losing is not an option for you. You start to see the world through a different lens, one that shows your true purpose and potential. Your true worth and value, and shows you who you really are. What you thought you could never do, now you start to do. Where you thought you could never go; now you begin to go. And the people you thought you would never meet, you will now begin to meet. When you start realizing your purpose, you start building the courage to step outside of your comfort zone. Or what some people call your *danger zone.* Stretch yourself beyond your old boundaries. Cross those lines that you never thought you could cross. There are people waiting for you to show up and give them what you've got. They are counting on you, and quite frankly, I am too.

You have to realize that everything you want is right on the other side of your comfort zone. Greatness, power, and impact do not live in comfort zones. In order to experience those things and to experience true purpose and potential, you have to step out of your comfort zone. Nothing great ever happened inside of a comfort zone. Remember those old lines you were afraid to cross or those ideas you were afraid to act on? Once you realize that you are Indispensable and that you were created for a purpose and for a reason, you have the freedom to do whatever you tell yourself you can do and to be whom you thought you could never be. Henry Ford said, *"Whether you think you can, or you think you can't – you're right."*

I once heard that if your dream does not scare you, then you are not dreaming big enough. There is greatness inside of you waiting to be unleashed and all you have to do is tap into it. Unlock the door and let it loose. What an awesome feeling it is to actually see yourself doing the things in life that you absolutely love to do but never did because you thought you were not capable of doing them. You may have been afraid to do so, or felt insignificant, so never even tried. Now is the time to turn your pain into passion. That drive will cause you to live an Indispensable life now! Who knows, you may even be able to turn your pain into a profit so that you can help others.

Action Steps

Are You Living Your True-life Purpose

✓   *What are my strengths?*

✓   *What makes me come alive?*

✓   *Am I aligned with my true inner self?*

✓   *Am I aligned with my passions and gifts?*

✓   *Am I aligned with my priorities and values?*

Take some time to think about these questions and if you can answer them truly and honestly, then you will be on your way to living a life full of purpose and potential. You will truly be living the Indispensable life now!

Scan the QR code below for a special video on living your true life purpose

JOSE FLORES

CHAPTER 5

Overcoming Your Fears

Fear can be the most crippling, unrelenting, paralyzing, and scary *emotion* you will ever experience if you let it. Growing up with a disability was not easy. One of my biggest fears as my body kept getting weaker and weaker was the fear of losing control of my body's strength and movement. First, it started getting harder for me to go up and down the stairs. Then, it started getting harder for me to get dressed and lift my arms above my head. My mind constantly had to adjust and adapt every time my body went through a new phase.

Can you imagine being able to walk and run and do different things and in the back of your mind knowing that someday soon, it will all come to an end? It was terrifying! My greatest fear was accepting that one day I would lose my ability to walk. Imagine turning 22 years old and thinking you are in your prime and life is just about to start for you. Life is going to be fun and amazing for you as you begin to explore it. Then, all of a sudden you lose your ability to walk and some of the things you use to do you can't do anymore. I'm sure you would feel like your life was over and ruined. That is exactly how I felt. I felt like there was no light at the end of the tunnel. It was so disheartening to me. I felt discouraged and embarrassed.

For many years I lived in fear, thinking of how people would look at me and treat me differently now that I was in a wheelchair. I would sometimes make up excuses to my friends (and even family members) for not going out because I did not want to deal with the stares and whispers of those watching me. I would say things like; I have a stomachache, I have to clean the house or my legs hurt. All kinds of excuses to try and get out of it and it always worked. Some of you reading right now, maybe even all of us, have felt like that before. The struggle is so overwhelming at times that it can make you lose hope. I was dwelling on the things that I no longer had control over and that I could no longer do.

Until one day I made a decision. I said, "If I have to live my life this way *for the time being*; I am going to make the best of it and I'm going to make the rest of my life the best of my life." I was able to overcome my fears and excuses by not focusing anymore on the things that I was not able to do and start focusing on the things that I **was** able to do. Having that type of outlook can really help you get through a lot of things and tough times when life comes at you.

****

The key is to focus on the "can do's" instead of the "can't do's"

****

Just as a side note, you don't have to be physically disabled to not be able to do things. People can be perfectly physically fit and still not be able to do certain things because of the different mental and emotional conditions that they suffer from. Such as depression, paranoia, low self-esteem, anxiety etc. The key is to focus on the "can do's" instead of the "can't do's." The can't do's will keep you locked up for a long time but the can do's gives you the freedom to focus on your abilities and your strengths in order to live the Indispensable life Now!

We have to understand that all fear comes from the mind. Whatever we tell ourselves is what we believe. What we believe, is what we will act upon. So what if we started telling ourselves something different when it comes to the things that we are fearful of?

When I graduated high school in 1995, I was still able to walk but my muscles were already starting to get weaker and give out on me. Our graduation ceremony was held in the back of our school on the football field. The bleachers were filled to capacity and there were even people standing on each side of the bleachers because there was no more room to sit. It was completely packed and the field was full that day. While all of us graduates were making our way towards the stage in the middle of the field we had to walk down a pretty steep hill to get there.

The entire time I was telling myself that my leg was going to give out on me and that I was going to fall in front of thousands of people. The butterflies in my stomach were going crazy. At this point in my life my legs would give out on me from time to time, and I would fall straight on the floor. I no longer had the strength to break the fall and hold myself up. Sometimes, I would really hurt myself. I was definitely full of fear that day. As I started getting closer and closer to the stage and they were getting ready to call my name, guess what happened to me? You guessed it! My right leg gave out on me and I fell on the floor in front of hundreds of people. The whole place went silent as I heard everyone take a gasp of air as they watched to see what happened to me and what I was going to do. They were all waiting to see if I was able to get up.

At that moment fear took complete control of me because of what I was telling myself in my head. Since I kept telling myself that my leg was going to give out on me, that is exactly what occurred. I want you to know that we have the power to speak life or death over any situation in our lives. We also have the power to speak things into existence, which is why we have to be very careful what we think and what we speak.

While I was on the floor I said to myself, what if I fake like I am really hurt so the paramedics would just carry me out of here and I would not have to see anybody or speak to anybody to explain what just happened to me. I was shocked and embarrassed and I had to make a critical decision. At that very moment, I decided to tell myself a different story. I started hearing this voice in my mind and it was saying, you better get up, you better finish this and you better go get that diploma! You have come way too far and worked way too hard to give up and miss out on this opportunity. Go and get what you've earned and deserve!

Can you believe this whole conversation I was having with myself was going on in my mind while I was still on the floor? It all happened in a few seconds but it felt like an eternity. It was so surreal. I felt like I was in a movie because everything was moving in slow motion as I looked around. As I started to get back up, the whole place was still in silence as one of my friends helped me up. When I finally got back on my feet everyone stood up, started clapping for me and cheering me on because I had decided not to give up. I told myself a different story and I overcame my fear.

Maybe if I had been telling myself a different story from the very beginning, this would not have happened to me. I would not have fallen down on the floor in front of thousands of people. I'm kind of glad smartphones and social media were not out back then because I believe it was one of those things that would have gone viral. It was so shocking; everyone would have been recording it and then sharing it!

The reality is fear is ever present, and it's what we tell ourselves that determines who wins. I continued to walk towards the principle and my guidance counselor, shook their hands, accepted my diploma and threw my cap in the air. One of the most embarrassing days in my life became one of the best and most memorable days of my life. Nowadays many people are fearful of so many different things. If they are on an airplane, they might be afraid of crashing. People are afraid of drowning so they stay away from any water. They do not take any risks or invest financially because they are afraid of losing their hard earned money. They won't invest in any relationships because they are fearful of getting hurt and the examples can go on and on.

****

Courage is not the absence of fear, but the overcoming of it

****

Your mind is telling you that you can't do it because you will fail or get hurt. The reality is, that is a lie. You do have the ability to do it, but since you are scared to move forward, you stay put and stay in your safe zone. Some fear is okay sometimes; because fear is what builds courage and you can't be courageous without fear. The only way to really overcome your fears once and for all is by facing your fears directly in the face and telling yourself a different story. Once you overcome that fear and it's gone, because you have conquered it, only one thing happens to you. You become victorious, you become the winner, and now that fear is gone you will be the only one remaining.

****

The "can't do's" will keep you locked up for a long time but the can do's gives you the freedom to focus on your abilities and your strengths in order to live the Indispensable life Now!

****

We have to remember that fear is a temporary emotion that cripples you momentarily as it scares you from moving forward. It prevents you from accomplishing what you wanted to accomplish or achieving what you wanted to achieve. It leaves you looking back and saying man, I missed the moment or that opportunity.

Many people believe that **F.E.A.R.** stands for **F**alse **E**vidence **A**ppearing **R**eal. Remember fear is not your reality. It's just an unpleasant emotion and you can overcome it. I would be brave enough to say that **F.E.A.R.** stands for **F**inding **E**xcuses **A**nd **R**easons not to do something that you really want to do. I personally think that **F.E.A.R** stands for **F**eeling **E**xcited **A**nd **R**eady or **F**ace **E**verything **A**nd **R**ise above it all victoriously!

Fear = Limitations
No Fear = *Endless Opportunities*

The problem is that we tend to listen to that little voice in our heads that tells us we do not have the power to do it and then we start to talk ourselves out of it. Or, we start to disqualify ourselves. The moment we do that we give fear the authority to take over and take control of the situation. However, if we activate courage we can overcome our fears. Courage is not the absence of fear, but the overcoming of it. So that means that you do whatever you have to do, to go around it, over it, (or the way I like to do it) and just go straight through it. The idea is to understand that fear tells you one thing but you have the power to tell yourself something different and conquer it! (*Remember the story of my graduation ceremony from high school.*)

Fear has no power over you unless you authorize it. If you give fear the permission to move forward in your mind the only thing you are doing is prolonging your opportunity to leave your mark on this world. I mentioned to you previously that my favorite book is the Bible and that is because it gives me so much encouragement, instruction, and inspiration.

In it, one of the scriptures says; "*we must take captive of every thought.*" This means we literally have the power to control our thoughts, what we think, and where we allow our minds to wander off. You can be thinking about one thing that could be allowing fear to rise up in your mind and at that very moment, you have the power to take control, refocus, and command your thought process to think about something else that will force the fear to submit. Force your fear to submit! All you need to do is learn how to use this special power that we all have.

You were created to be phenomenal and nothing less. How many times have you tried to do something to express yourself through some sort of creative idea, thought, verbal opinion, or action and wound up talking yourself out of it because you allowed fear to grip you? Then, later on, thought about how you just missed your opportunity to make a difference or an impact and you beat yourself up about it? Has it ever happened to you? It has happened to me many times.

At one of my old jobs, we were collectively thinking about ways to improve certain processes in our quarterly meeting. In my mind, I had a great idea. I wanted to create an easy to use form for customers to fill out when they needed to close their accounts. We had a form in place but it was very confusing and we would have to make countless calls to customers to help them correctly fill out the form. At the meeting, I did not verbalize my idea because I allowed fear to keep my mouth shut.

A few weeks later I created the much-needed form. My new form provided less confusion for the customers and fewer callbacks on our end. This would result in saving the company time and money. Yet, I hesitated initially. The new form could have been implemented weeks earlier had I just spoken up, but I did not because of fear and I missed my opportunity. Thankfully, I did not waste too much time and made the revised form. I was able to make a difference on both ends of the spectrum.

****
Force your fear to submit
****

I was fortunate that my manager at the time thought it was a great idea. She allowed me to implement it and share it with the team, but those missed opportunities do not always come around twice. Remember that when fear tries to raise its ugly little head, conquer it by being brave, activating courage, and taking a chance on yourself. You can save yourself and your team member's valuable time and money by winning over fear. Be relentless with your creativity and your bravery and always stand up for what you believe in! I want you to repeat after me and say to yourself right now, fear has no future in my future! Come on, say it again and say it with boldness, say it with conviction, and say it like you mean it! Your life is depending on you. The truth is that the only person you need to convince is yourself. All fear does, every day, everywhere and to everyone is to stop him or her from fulfilling their passion in their lives and making a difference. But once fear knows that you believe in yourself and you have the courage to stand up to it, it has a very slim to none chance of having defeated you successfully. Say it again one more time, fear has no future in my future!

Fear cannot win over faith and courage. These two elements are just too strong for fear to come against them. Whenever you feel fear coming after you, remember your belief system, then put on courage and I promise you that you will always come out the victor and always come out on top! When it comes to fear we only have two options. We can either shrink back and let fear win or we can stampede forward and overcome it. Which one will you choose?

Action Steps

Overcoming Fear

➤ *Be Courageous, Bold, and Brave.*

➤ *Turn your fear into conquering energy.*

➤ *Believe in yourself; know that you can do it.*

➤ *Take a chance on yourself and trust in YOU!*

➤ *Face your fears with strength, be upfront and direct and take control*

➤ *Know that F.E.A.R. means Face Everything And Rise.*

➤ *Think about one thing every day that scares you and DO IT!*

Scan the QR code below for a special video on overcoming fear

CHAPTER 6
The Power of Showing Up

Statistics show that 85% of success comes from just showing up. However, I want to let you know that before you can show up for anything in life, you first have to wake up. Not only figuratively speaking but also literally. You have to wake up and realize that life is too short to stay in sleep mode. There's too much life going on! There are tons of opportunities that you will miss out on if you remain in sleep mode all day.

There are people that are getting cheated by you not waking up, getting up, and showing up with what you have to offer. I know sometimes the thought of showing up can be a little intimidating because you may be thinking that you are going to be around other people that are smarter than you, are more successful than you, and are more influential than you are. Even though that may all be true, you shouldn't let that stop you from showing up anyway. There is somebody out there that needs only what you can give. Don't ever think that the gift you have to offer is too small to make a huge impact.

You may not be the smartest person in the world, or you may not have the greatest level of education or have a large influence on people currently, but trust me when I tell you this; when you start to show up, the things that you never imagined could be possible start happening for you. You begin to make a difference, you begin to make an impact in the lives of others, and then your sphere of influence begins to grow larger and larger all because you choose to show up.

****
Statistics show that 85% of success comes from just showing up
****

The very term, "showing up" seems simple. You just show up right? Actually, it involves much more than that. I will give you specific ways to show up, make a difference and get seen, but first, I want to share a story with you. The story is a bit lengthy, but walk the journey with me and in the end, you will see how all the pieces of the puzzle align together to create an even bigger picture and all because I decided to show up.

One night while scrolling through my Facebook feed, I came upon a free Get Motivated Seminar event that was coming to Fort Lauderdale Florida. The main speaker was none other than the great Les Brown. It was a free event and after being a little skeptical about it, I decided to register. Since I was an up and coming speaker I figured it would be a great opportunity to connect and network with like-minded people in the industry.

A major part of showing up requires *preparation*. The night before the seminar my wife and I were up late getting my speaker packages together. We were ready to give the packages to several people at the event with the hopes of just getting out there and potentially getting some speaking engagements. The day of the seminar we woke up at 5 o'clock in the morning to get to the seminar by 6:30

a.m. They started letting people in at 7:00 a.m. and we wanted to make sure we were able to get good seats.

When we arrived, there were thousands of people waiting to get in. We got in line to get our seats right away. They started promptly at 8:00 a.m. The host of the event came on stage to get the crowd going and when I tell you that this guy was so funny, he had everybody laughing, feeling good, and comfortable immediately. There were so many great speakers that were there.

My wife noticed that after every speaker completed their speech, they would go out to the lobby to meet and greet the people. My wife, being the brilliant woman that she is said, "Honey, you should go out to the lobby too and give your speaker kit to the speakers. You never know who you could meet and what connections you might be able to make." So we both went to the back of the lobby to get something to drink and network through the crowd of people.

The host happened to be walking by and my wife said, "Honey, you should give him a package!" Since I was a little nervous and intimidated by being around all of these prominent figures, I tried to play it off and said, "Nah, he's just the host." Thank God for my wife though! (Men, this is why we need a good woman by our side) She said, "Baby, don't you know that the host goes backstage with all the other millionaire speakers?" Once she said that, it was like a light bulb went off in my head and I said, "Yeah you're right baby!" However, by this time he already passed us and I thought, man, I just missed my opportunity.

I felt terrible because here I was, doing the very thing that a lot of people have done to me in the past and still do at times. I was diminishing his position and his potential as just being "*the host*" of the event. So my wife said, I'm going to the restroom and I will be right back. While she was in the restroom I was beating myself up because of what just happened. All of a sudden I looked to my right and I saw the host coming back my way and said to myself, I am not going to miss my opportunity this time. I saw him through my peripheral coming right towards me and he says, "Hey bud, how are you enjoying yourself? Do you think I'm funny, am I doing a good job?" I knew he was just joking but I said absolutely, you are hilarious, seriously, and he really was! He asked me what brought me to the Get Motivated Seminar and I said I'm an up and

JOSE FLORES

coming speaker and I came to learn, grow, and connect with people. He said, "Do you have a business card?" I said, "Yes absolutely! I actually have a speaker kit with all of my information and a DVD of my story. Can I give you a copy?" He said, sure I will actually go backstage and give it to the CEO of Get Motivated. Now I can't promise you anything but you never know what can happen (Let us not forget that my wife had just said that very statement a few minutes earlier.)

****
There are people that are getting cheated by you not waking up, getting up, and showing up with what you have to offer
****

So I said well let me give you two then, one for him and one for you. He said, yeah man you have such a great smile and I can see the joy in you. There are so many people out here who are not in a wheelchair, walking around here like their life is over and looking grumpy. Yet here you are smiling like there is nothing wrong with you and I like that. I said, thanks for the compliment. I'm just trying to make a difference wherever I can. He said, cool

106

I've got to run because I have to go back on stage to introduce the next speaker. I'll see you around.

Before we continue further into the story, so far we have seen that the power of showing up involves being prepared, putting a smile on your face, and looking for opportunities. Recall that I went out to where the speakers were and introduced myself. As you network and show up to different events, make yourself available to be seen. Have a great attitude, be prepared, smile, and search out any potential opportunities. Having a smile can make a huge difference. People are naturally attracted to happy people. When people see me in the wheelchair and then see this big smile on my face it usually encourages others to recognize that life can be hard at times, but you can still choose to be happy. When you can put a smile on your face, in the face of adversity, it speaks volumes to people. It tells them hey, if he can do it then so can I.

After the host left, I was in shock and filled with so much excitement I could barely contain myself. Right after he left my wife comes out of the restroom and I am just beside myself. She can tell by the look on my face that something major just happened. I said to her, "Honey, you will not believe what just happened!" So I started telling her how the interaction went, and like every other woman in the world, she said, "Wait, wait, wait, I want details!" While I continued telling her all the details about what happened, I see the host walking quickly towards us again just minutes later. He comes up to us and says, Hey, I just gave your speaker kit to the CEO. Can you stay after the event so I can introduce you to him? I said, are you kidding me? Absolutely!

At this point, my wife and I were so excited that we felt like screaming at the top of our lungs. We stayed until the end of the event to meet the CEO. I was also trying to see if I could meet Les Brown to give him a copy of my speaker kit as well. I wasn't able to meet Les Brown but as everyone started to leave I saw the host come out from backstage with the CEO. The host introduces me to the CEO and he says, Hi, I saw you earlier and noticed that smile on your face, don't you ever lose that smile! I said, "I get that a lot, thank you." (The funny thing is that when we first arrived at the Broward Convention Center in Fort Lauderdale Florida my wife says; honey, make sure you're always smiling because you never know who is watching.)

After telling the CEO about myself and that I'm a public speaker, he said, can you come to the Get Motivated tour next week in West Palm Beach Florida? I said, yes I can. He then says, great! I will give you ten minutes on stage to show me what you've got! I said, "Are you serious?" With a big smile on his face, he said yes, just come to the registration table the day of the event, ask for me and they will take care of you. I said, so is this a confirmation? You definitely want me to come by next week and speak? I still could not believe it. He said, yes it's confirmed and it was a pleasure meeting you. We shook hands and we both left. When my wife and I got in the car we both looked at each other in amazement and said God is so good. We started screaming and crying at the same time because we were filled with so much joy and excitement that day.

****

Once you are present and you've given other people the chance to be exposed to you, that is when the law of attraction kicks in and the power of proximity is released

****

One of the main things you need to do when showing up to any event is to be prepared. Be very prepared. I was given an opportunity to speak on a world-class business tour in front of thousands of people all because I showed up, had a smile on my face, was prepared, and searched out the opportunities! I was only a couple of months into my career as a speaker. To be given this opportunity was huge!

I read a quote from Whitney Young Jr. that says, "*It is better to be prepared for an opportunity and not have one, then to have an opportunity and not be prepared*" and I was prepared! You need to be prepared not only physically but also mentally. Be prepared to engage and to have conversations with those that are around you. It's called Networking! By networking, you are positioning yourself to meet someone who may be able to take your career to the next level. You might make a connection with someone who can help turn your dreams into a reality. Make sure you are prepared everywhere you go because you will never know when an opportunity will present itself.

The power of showing up is just that, *Showing Up*! Just being there and being present can make all the difference in the world. Once you are present and you have given other people the chance to be exposed to you, that is when the law of attraction kicks in and the power of proximity is released. The power of proximity simply means being around other like-minded people or being around other people that are already successful at doing what it is that you also desire to do. And then just start doing what they are doing. There's no reason to reinvent the wheel. There is an old saying that says "if it isn't broke, don't fix it." Imagine a football player going to a basketball practice and trying to do the same drills he does at football practice. Those basketball players would be severely hurt and would never make it. The point is if the system is already working don't try to change it.

In order for someone to be attracted to you and for the law of attraction to kick in, they have to be aware of you and around you. The only way for people to be aware of you and around you is for you to show up! By showing up you give people the chance to know you and then grow to like you.

We left the Broward Convention Center at 7 p.m. and headed to the Hyatt hotel right across the street. One of the main speakers named Willie Jolley, who really inspired me, was having a private meet and greet there. The presentation was finished around 9 p.m. and my wife and I stood afterward to meet personally with Willie and his wife, Dee. I shared with him a little bit about what I was doing and where I wanted to go in my speaking career and he said that there was something about my spirit that he was drawn to. (By the way, he also mentioned my smile as well.) I told him I wanted to ask him a question and I knew it was a long shot. He had a very busy schedule and was in high demand, but I asked him if he wouldn't mind mentoring me, giving me some guidance, and advice about the speaking business. I said this with confidence and boldness, but with the utmost respect and humility. I had never met him before. I've watched his presentations online but never met him personally and he certainly did not know who I was. It was a long shot indeed. He looked directly into my eyes and said that he would be honored to mentor me! I knew that I needed to surround myself with greatness! I also knew that in order to be great, I couldn't stop moving forward. On the contrary, when I feel like I want to give up, that is when I keep going.

I could have been satisfied with the opportunity from Get Motivated to speak in front of thousands of people. At that point, I was already sitting in my wheelchair for 14 hours. It would have been easy, and valid for me to just go home. I could have skipped the meet and greet with Willie Jolley but again I say, greatness does not stop. Greatness is not a destination but a constant drive to seek out every opportunity. Had I skipped the meet and greet I would have missed my opportunity to be mentored by a great speaker who would later come to give me valuable insight into the business.

****
By showing up you give people the chance to get to know you and then grow to like you
****

Before we left we took pictures with Willie and his wife Dee and I bought a signed copy of his bestselling book "A Setback is a Setup for a Comeback." He asked for my information and gave me his information as well. We have stayed in touch ever since. He calls me from time to time when he and his wife Dee are in town so we can get together for dinner. He has also given me valuable lessons and insider tips on how to increase my speaking engagements and turn my passion into profit. This all occurred because I was willing to go the extra mile to attend his event, waited until everyone left to meet with him personally and took a chance to ask a question that no one else in the room was willing to ask. I'm sure that there were people in the room who wanted to ask him to be their mentor as well, but for whatever reason, those people told themselves in their mind that it was not possible and they let fear win.

****
Greatness is not a destination but a constant drive to seek out every opportunity
****

We all have opportunities presented to us; however, many of us do not embrace the opportunities that are present and we miss out. Worst yet, we delay our success and greatness because we did not act on the opportunity. I also met other people at Willie Jolley's event that would later help further my career as well. My life changed forever on December 3, 2015 and I will never forget it.

I've added a flow chart below so you can visualize how this all transpired. As we move along in the story, I will add more to the chart and in the end, you will get to see how all of this came full circle.

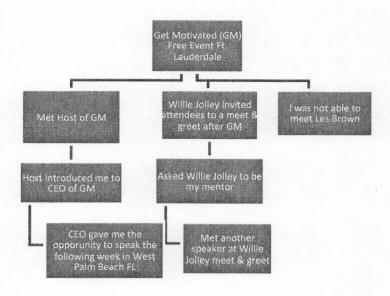

The following week Wednesday, December 9, 2015 West Palm Beach Convention Center in West Palm Beach, Florida

This week was the same routine as the last week. We woke up early, got the speaker kits ready and headed to

West Palm Beach. We got there pretty early and it was already packed again. I guess the word had spread about how good the event was the week before in Fort Lauderdale because it seemed like there were several hundred more people at this event. My wife and I arrived at the registration table and asked for the CEO. The security guard says the CEO will not be here today. My wife's heart sank and I start getting a little worried. I asked if the host was there. The security guy says who can I tell him is looking for him? I said, "Tell him its Jose Flores." The security guy radios for the host and tells him that I am here. The host comes to the front and says; what took you so long buddy and brings us to our seats.

We immediately get backstage access. I am in awe because I'm now hanging out with all the same millionaire speakers that were there the previous week in Fort Lauderdale. It was amazing! Last week I was an attendee, and this week I am on the stage! The power of showing up!

My wife and I and our videographer are all looking at each other like, is this really happening? There were roughly 3,500 people in attendance that day. I was having mixed emotions. A little nervous and excited at the same time because this was the largest group of people I have ever spoken in front of at this point in my career. So you already know that the butterflies, better yet, the entire zoo was having a meeting in my stomach as I am preparing and praying before it's my turn to go on.

Around noon, the host says, Jose, you're up! It was one of the most exciting and terrifying moments of my life. He says, listen Jose I apologize, but we were not able to get the ramp here with enough time to get you on stage. What I am going to do is have you come down from the back of the room to the front of the stage so everyone can see you.

I will come down to the front of the stage while I am introducing you. As he is introducing me he tells everyone how we met the prior week at the Fort Lauderdale seminar and how he noticed the smile on my face and found out that I was a motivational speaker. He told the crowd how he introduced me to the CEO of Get Motivated and how the CEO thought it would be a good idea if I came through today to share a little bit of my story and encourage them.

As I made my way down the aisle I asked the audience; are you guys fired up? In which they all responded with a big YEAH! Everyone began to clap and the synergy was amazing. I knew I only had ten minutes to bring my A-game and give it all I had. As I shared my story I could see that the people were mesmerized with how I ended up in the wheelchair, how I have overcome and how I still have to overcome every day. They were tuned in. Every eye was watching me as I moved from side to side.

When I was done motivating and encouraging them to follow their dreams and not let anything stop them from achieving their best no matter what life throws at them, the crowd gave me a standing ovation. The feeling that I had after that point was indescribable! In that moment I realized, beyond a shadow of a doubt, that I was moving in my purpose. The fact that I knew that I could motivate people to reach beyond their current circumstances was what I wanted to do for the rest of my life.

I then went backstage to see if Les Brown was still there so I could try again to give him my speaker kit. I missed him in Fort Lauderdale the week before. I thought surely I would get to meet him now since I have backstage access, but they said that he had already left because he had another event to go to at the Sun Life Stadium in Miami Florida, where the Miami Dolphins play. Now let me rewind a little bit. The week before at Willie Jolley's meet and greet I also met a man who is an author and a motivational speaker. We exchanged information at the event and stayed in touch all week. He called me the night before the Get Motivated event in West Palm Beach to tell me that he was speaking at an event and had extra tickets and wanted to invite my wife and I to come see him speak. I told him I was speaking at the Get Motivated event but would swing by his event afterward if time permitted. The event that he happened to be speaking at was also at the Sun Life Stadium in Miami. That's right, the same event that Les Brown was going to be speaking at. I thought to myself, this has got to be a God moment. I said this could be my opportunity to finally catch up with Les to give him my speaker kit and information. I missed him in Fort Lauderdale, I missed him in West Palm Beach, now I was being given another opportunity in Miami, to not only watch my new friend speak but also meet my mentor, Les Brown.

After rubbing elbows with some people in the lobby, meeting different people, and exchanging information, we left the West Palm Beach Convention Center and made our way down to Miami. When we arrived at the Stadium and got to the club level I see my friend and thank him for inviting us to the event. He immediately starts introducing me to all these other successful speakers in the industry. I just met this guy last week and here he was inviting me to this event and introducing me to all these people. All this was happening so quickly, all within a one-week period. When it comes to grabbing hold of your dreams, make sure you stop at nothing until you get it. I had been praying and asking God to open all the doors and for Him to do the impossible for me but let me tell you, He was moving fast!

As I was sitting at that event and listening to all these different speakers at the Sun Life Stadium, I looked to my left and saw Les Brown walking our way. There was a bunch of people saying hi to him and taking a lot of pictures of him and with him. He made eye contact with me and I asked if I could take a picture with him too. He said, absolutely! While we were taking the picture I start telling him how I have been trying to catch up with him since the morning in West Palm Beach and how I had been chasing him through three different counties over the course of a week. I told him that I also spoke in West Palm Beach at Get Motivated. Then he said, I thought you looked familiar. Were you sitting in the middle, right up front? I said, yes sir I was. I then asked him if I could give him my speaker kit and he said yes absolutely.

Earlier in the morning in West Palm Beach, Les Brown stated that he was looking for 21 protégés to train and mentor. When I met him I told him that I was *hungry* and that I wanted to be one of his 21 protégés. He chuckled and asked me if my contact information was in the package in case he wanted to contact me. I said, yes sir it is. Everything you need to reach me is in there for you!

The very next day was a Thursday, a normal day just like any other. I was at work processing everything that happened within the last seven days. I was pondering on the amazing experiences I had and how I was finally able to meet my mentor the great Les Brown. While I was at work, I received a phone call from a number that I did not recognize. I thought that it might have been someone that I had given my card to who was just following up with me. When I picked up the call I said hello; and the person on the other line said, hello can I speak to Jose? I said yes, this is he, and to whom am I speaking with? The person on the line said hello Jose, this is Les Brown how are you doing?

I almost fell out of my wheelchair! I was filled with so much joy and excitement. I could not believe that he called me the very next day and I was on the phone with the legendary Les Brown. He asked me several questions to get to know me and told me that he would like to work with me and that he could help me reach my goals. We have been in touch ever since and have been working on some amazing things together.

The purpose of me sharing the entire detailed story with you is to give you a bird's eye view of all of the events that transpired. Sometimes we are so afraid to move forward because we cannot see the full picture of where we will end up or we don't know what our next step is going to be. You don't always have to see the next step. You just need to be persistent, consistent, and insistent on moving forward to get to where you want to be.

None of this would have ever happened if I did not SHOW UP! I had the honor and privilege of actually being introduced and speaking on the same stage, side by side, with Les Brown himself at the same Get Motivated event that I meet him at, less than 1 year later. Les Brown invited me to speak to the audience about not letting your struggle become your standard and not giving up on your dreams. The reason I am telling you all of this is to let you know that when you show up, you give your dreams a better chance of becoming the reality that you are seeking. So keep on waking up, getting up, and showing up, and make sure that you never give up!

So many grand opportunities have resulted in my life because of the power of showing up. See the completed flowchart of how everything was linked together in this story. So what is it that's holding you back? There is no excuse. You have what it takes this very moment to turn your dreams into a reality and you can start by showing up. For me, it started with a free Get Motivated event and less than 1 year later, I was side-by-side speaking with my mentor Les Brown on stage at the same Get Motivated event in Miami Florida. Since then I have been on tour with Les Brown and traveled the world speaking to thousands of people on the importance of never giving up, and never letting their struggle become their standard. Les is not only my mentor but my friend. I have learned so much from him and I'm proud to be called his mentee!

The Power of Showing Up - Flow Chart

Action Steps

The Power of Showing Up

> ➤ *Wake up!*

> ➤ *Dress up!*

> ➤ *Show up!*

> ➤ *Be prepared!*

> ➤ *Always Smile!*

> ➤ *Never give up!*

> ➤ *Seek out the opportunities!*

> ➤ *Be expecting great things to happen!*

Scan the QR code below for a special video on the power of showing up

CHAPTER 7
Mind Management

The most effective mindset is one that takes advantage of every current resource and opportunity that is available and uses it to make a positive change not only in his/her own life but also in the lives of others. I have found that most young people think that their best is yet to come. Many older people believe that their best was back in the "good ole days," or has already passed. Yet, many people miss the opportunity to live their best life NOW!

There is a story about two twin boys that were raised by an abusive father. One grew up to also be an abusive adult and when he was asked what happened to cause him to be this way he said, "I watched my father."

129

The other brother grew up and never became abusive. When he was asked what happened, he also said, "I watched my father." Two boys from the same father had two different mindsets and perspectives. It is a choice, and the choice is yours.

As I mentioned earlier, before my mindset shift, I used to believe and think that I would never be capable of doing anything great or significant in life. I was always focusing on the things I could not do. That was the story I kept telling myself over and over, and guess what? I never did do anything great. It wasn't until I made up my mind to do something great that opportunities started coming into my life. If you can believe it, then you can receive it and achieve it. I started to recognize that I have the power to control my own thought process and thought patterns. I could tell myself whatever story I chose to tell myself. I think that Abraham Lincoln said it best when he said, *"We can complain because rose bushes have thorns, or we can rejoice because thorn bushes have roses."* Life has a lot to do with perception and how we decide to look at the things around us. Is the glass half empty or half full? What do you think? I personally believe that life would look a whole lot different to many of us if we were to look at life and perceive it not as it is, but as it could be.

Affirmations are also a huge plus in regards to what we think about ourselves. Whether we think of them in our minds or whether we speak them out loud, they must be done. If you can start learning to affirm yourself every day and say things like; I believe I am worthy of what I desire, and today I am ready to receive it. You will start to see a drastic change in the way things begin to happen in your favor. Situations and circumstances in life begin to minimize and fade away as you start getting a clearer vision. Have a vision of what it is you want in life and where it is you want to go. By affirming yourself you are, essentially, giving yourself a permission slip to be more of your true self. Affirmations, when used correctly, can also help you reprogram your subconscious mind for success.

****
If you can believe it, then you can receive it, and achieve it
****

In the best-selling book of all time, the Bible, it talks about two great principles, along with many others that have to deal with the mind. The first one says, *as a man thinks, so he becomes.* The second one says, *do not be conformed to this world but be transformed by the renewing of your mind.*

So what does that mean for you? In other words, you are what you think you are. Whatever you are thinking, you are becoming or you will become. Whatever you focus on the longest becomes the strongest. I want to ask you a serious question that I really want you to think about. What is it that you have been focusing on or thinking about that you have been making stronger in your life today? What are the dreams and goals that you want to accomplish but have put them on hold for one reason or another?

****
Affirmations, when used correctly, can also help you reprogram your subconscious mind for success
****

Ask yourself these questions:

➢ *Am I at peace and joyful with where I am?*

➢ *Am I content and happy with what I am doing?*

➢ *Is it positive, productive, and profitable for me?*

➢ *Am I making a difference and an impact in the lives of others?*

If you answered yes to any of these questions then you may be on the right track to reaching the level of success that you are willing to work for. But if you answered no, then you need to make a radical change in your thinking and actions. It may be time to start focusing on some new things in your life a lot longer than you have been. Begin by focusing on more positive thoughts and the questions above, so you can find a new strength and create a new path.

****

Whatever you focus on the longest becomes the strongest

****

We all go through struggles at some point or another in our lives. In life, we can't always control what happens to us but what we can control is how we react when life happens. It means we have to think about how we are going to react to the situation and get through it. Renew your mind by the way you are thinking.

A question that I frequently get asked, especially by kids, is how do I get dressed in the morning? I tell them that every morning my wife or one of my children have to get me dressed in the bed. After that, one of them has to physically lift me up to put me in my wheelchair just so I am able to start my day. I then tell them that after they lift me up to put me in my wheelchair, it is up to me to lift myself up mentally. I have to prepare myself mentally to be in my wheelchair for sometimes up to sixteen hours a day and sometimes more than that.

The process requires me to make sure that every day I am in the proper state of mind to be able to endure the struggle that comes along with having to be in my wheelchair that long. What are your struggles? What obstacles do you have to remove from your thought process to succeed in your day? Is it insecurity, pride, anxiety, fear of failure, fear of success, arrogance, or maybe self-pity? Take control, and command your mind every day to always have an attitude of gratitude and to be in a state of gratefulness at all times. Even though I am in a wheelchair, I am very grateful that I am living an abundant life and I have the opportunity to make an impact in other people's lives every day. Ask yourself "what is my why?" Your **_why_** is the reason that you get out of bed every morning. Your reason why will fuel you to do what needs to be done on a daily basis. For many people, their wife and/or kids are the reason why they work so hard and grind every day. Others dream about the difference they can make financially in the lives of their parents (buying them a home to retire in, paying off their debt etc...). Others get their "whys" from being told they will never be great or successful so they use the hate and negativity from others to push them to hustle every day. Others simply want to be the BEST version of themselves that they can be and as a result, they turn that self-motivating desire into their "why."

Whatever your "why" is, keep it in the front of your mind. Write it down, make the vision clear. Keep your "why" in a place where you can see it every day. Just like the affirmations, if you need to write it down on a piece of paper and place it in your bathroom, car, or wallet, do it. Wherever you place them, just be sure to look at them every day and say them every day.

It may seem like no big deal but successful people know their "why." They can tell you their morning "ritual" every day and what affirmations they use daily to pump themselves up. When things are not going your way, when the breakthrough seems like it's not coming, when the opportunities seem non-existent. What you are telling yourself every day will be the difference on whether or not the success you desire in life will be something you thought about and then gave up on, or something that you actually accomplish. In other words, you are what you say you are. You can have what you desire to have. You can achieve what you believe you can achieve. You will be surprised at your energy level when you have a why behind what you do and what you want in life.

I was recently having a conversation with my friend Keith. I was sharing with him that when my body goes through a change and I get a little weaker, I have to learn how to adapt to the new change; figure out new ways to do things. For example, a couple of years ago, I could open a 20oz soda bottle with no problem. Now, because my muscles have gotten weaker, I had to learn to use my teeth to open the bottle. Most of you don't have to use your teeth to open a bottle. You use your hands and never think twice about it. Unfortunately, these are the "little" things that others can do so easily that I cannot. Then Keith said something that I thought was so profound and fits perfectly with mind management. He said, "It's not only about adapting to the changes and learning new ways to do things but more importantly about having the mental ability to overcome and push through the changes." He leaned in a little closer and said with conviction, "Jose, you are a mental beast, you are so strong mentally and other people need to know how you do it!" That is exactly what this chapter is about. I want you to become a mental beast! When you overcome the mind, you can overcome anything!

****
Successful people know their "why." They can tell you their morning ritual every day and what affirmations they use daily to pump themselves up
****

Take control of your thoughts today. Successful people don't walk around feeling sorry for what they do not have. Instead, they make the day their puppet. Picture a puppet on a string and imagine that your actions are being controlled by your thoughts. Your mindset, thoughts, and perspective control the actions you take every day. If you want to live the Indispensable Life now, learn to control your mindset, your thoughts, your perspective and you will master the day. Let negative thoughts control you and it will control every action you do throughout the day. People go years being controlled by negative thoughts. They are puppets on strings of negativity, fear, and self-doubt. Trust me, I know because I used to be one of them. I'm not talking as if I have not been in this very place. I have and I never want to be controlled like that again. It is a daily choice. I visualize the puppet and say to myself, "Am I going to be controlled by negative strings or positive ones today?" Am I going to be controlled by fear or by courage? Am I going to be controlled by self-doubt or am I going to believe in myself today? If your actions are being controlled by negative strings start to change your thought process right now. I believe in you. Say your affirmations every day, find your why, and control your thoughts. Be grateful, be positive, and keep working hard on those goals. You can do it! I know you can.

We have all heard it said that your attitude (which is what you think) determines your altitude (which is how high and far you can go) and I have found that statement to be very true. There are times that I don't feel like getting out of bed because my body feels weak due to my situation but then I have to remember that I don't live my life based off of my feelings. Rather, I choose to live my life based on my purpose. That is the mindset that I personally try to put on every day. Is it easy? No! It wasn't easy at first but I had to learn to train the brain. Just like you go to the gym to work out your muscles so you can get strong, the same is true for your brain. You have to train it, exercise it, and expand it so it can get strong and stay strong to handle the weight of life when life throws you a curve ball.

Every thought that comes to life has to travel through the mind first before it ever becomes a reality. That is why it is so important to continually be in a positive and creative state of mind. So the question that I want to ask you is this; have you been expanding the vision of yourself lately? A vision is just a picture of where you see yourself going. What thoughts have you allowed to cross your mind, what story have you been telling yourself? Hopefully, you've been telling yourself things like; I am going to make it to the other side, I will arrive at the place that I have been heading towards, and I will be a success.

Having the proper mindset is critical in being successful at working towards turning your dreams into a reality and living the type of life that you have always wanted. This world is so full of negative things that are constantly competing for our attention. It is a distraction that tries to make you lose focus of what your vision and mission are. We have the control over what we allow to enter into our mind, ears, and eyes. Be very careful of what you are thinking, what you are listening to and what you are watching. Your subconscious mind is soaking it all in.

****
Train the brain
****

You may have heard of that old saying, "What you put in is what will come out." So if you are thinking negatively or around negative people that are draining you, more than likely you will become frustrated and let off negative energy. But if you are around positive people who are building you up, not tearing you down, and thinking about positive things, then more than likely you will be in a good state of mind. You will let off that same energy but this time in a positive way. You might be thinking about your current situation right now, maybe even a past situation or whatever "thing" that you're going through. Whatever the struggle is, it can be hindering you from getting to your future destination. I recommend you shake it off, think about where you are going, make sure your shoes are strapped, keep pressing forward and remember your "why". We should all learn to be using our past experiences, past fears, and past ups and downs, along with both the good and bad to fuel our passion for getting launched into the next level.

"Sometimes we have to soak ourselves in the tears and fears of the past, to water our future gardens."– Suzy Kassem.

The power of the mind is huge because you can literally think yourself in or out of the type of mindset that you choose. It is a choice and you have the authority and power to command it. Choose wisely not only for yourself but also for those who love and care about you and that are counting on you to make the right decisions. If you are thinking about big things happening in your life and you are working towards them, then eventually big things will happen for you. On the flip side of that coin, if you are thinking about small things happening in your life then more than likely small things will happen for you, especially if you're not putting in the work.

My friend and mentor Les Brown says *"the reason most people are not successful in life is not because they aim to high and miss, NO! It is because they aim to low and HIT."* OUCH! When I heard that I was shocked because that statement is so true for many people. It saddens me when I see a person full of potential and not holding themselves to a higher standard in life. They are not utilizing their God-given gifts to achieve top-level success. The reality is that most people die leaving liabilities and not legacies. Too often, they never thought they could do it or didn't have the courage to. If you are reading this book, I know that you want to leave a legacy and I want you to start today moving towards it.

Everyone would like to achieve some level of success in life. The thing that you have to determine is what does success look like for you and how can you work on making it a reality? You may have a certain mindset about success based off of the way that you grew up, your environment, or what you may have seen on TV and movies. This may or may not be an accurate mindset about success. What I mean is that we don't know what we don't know and the sad part is that we don't even know that we don't know it. Unless someone tells you or you get exposed to it, you would not have known otherwise.

I have met several people, who came up to me after I spoke, and tell me how they grew up in a poverty mentality culture. They were raised in a culture where success was not even talked about. Life was to be lived to get by, make ends meet, and just be satisfied with what life gave them. Their grandparents, and parents lived mediocre lives and they were taught to do the same. It was not until those individuals made a choice to expand their knowledge that they came across all the greatness a life of abundance brings. In our technology advanced world, there are so many opportunities to learn and grow. They started to follow the people who they desired to be like on social

143

media. They watched videos of the people who were doing what they wanted to do. They researched how to get started in the business. For many of them, what started as a personal quest for growth caused their entire life to be shifted. Their mindset was changed and they saw a vision for their life that they just had to accomplish.

****

The reality is that most people die leaving liabilities and not legacies

****

So how do you know if the mindset you have is a correct one? The answer is, if whatever success looks like to you makes you content, happy, and full of joy then you have become successful in life. If you are looking at your life, and you have this gut feeling that there is more to life than "just this", you may want to reevaluate your goals.

Success can look different to different people and just because someone else has a different mindset about success does not mean that the one you have is any more or less, it's only different. That is why it's never good to compare someone else's success to your own. Some people may look successful financially and materially but they are not successful in their happiness, joy, nor at peace in their hearts, so is that real success? This is something for you to think about.

As a kid, I was always told that I can do whatever I put my mind to and I know you may have heard it before as well. Why do you think they use that saying? Not because it's just a saying, but because it actually holds some measure of truth. Many of us are not where we want to be in life because we do not think that we can get there so we never even try to set out on the journey. We defeat ourselves mentally and talk ourselves out of it before we even give it a shot. In our minds, we disqualify ourselves. All because of a small simple negative thought in our mind. Even though it was just a negative thought, you have allowed it to become your reality because you thought it into existence. In other words, you already made it happen in your mind before it became a reality. WOW! Take a moment and think about that; it was deep right? It may take some time for you to digest that last statement. It's okay, take your time, there is no rush, the book is all yours.

I have always been an affectionate person ever since I was a little kid. By that I mean, when I greeted

145

people I would always hug or kiss them, give them a high five, handshake, or a pat on the back. I have always been very outgoing and energetic. However, the weaker my body started becoming the less I was able to do some of those things. It was a special kind of love that was built inside of me. There are days where I miss doing those things.

There would be times where I would tell my wife, I wish I could stand up and kiss you, or I wish I could wrap my arms around you and hold you tight and she would say, "I know baby, I know, but it's okay, we make it work." If I continually focused on the negative thoughts, my marriage would be a disaster. I would be so miserable about myself, that my marriage would fall apart. Yet, my wife says the thing she admires about me most is my strong mental state. I refuse to be the puppet on negative strings.

I remember my wife and I were watching a Tony Robbins documentary called "I am not your guru." There was a part of the documentary where it shows Tony prepping himself and getting himself mentally prepared to address the crowd. He would run up the stage steps, swing his arms around in the air, pound his chest like a beast, and then take the stage. He was psyching himself out, filling himself with positive energy to transfer that same energy to the audience. The energy in the room was amazing.

Since I am not able to do those same physical things any longer, I had to learn to train my brain. I had to learn how to psych myself mentally by thinking about positive things and building up my own energy level. When I get on stage, I want to deliver an explosive presentation and come out on fire right from the door. You don't have to have the same method as someone else to be successful. There are tons of different ways to do the same thing. The new invention, the new business, the new product is waiting on you. Sure, something similar may already be out there, but what spin or new method of delivery can you put on it. What ideas are in your thoughts?

Your mindset and perspective in life will determine your destination. Your thoughts become your reality. So again I ask you, what have you been thinking about? It may be time to change your thought process or your thought patterns and grab a hold of the Indispensable life you want to live and deserve. I personally THINK you can do it!

147

Matter of fact, I know you can do it. If I can do it, with all the physical limitations I have, I know you can do it. I believe in you! Now get it done!

Here is a simple and easy acronym to help you remember Mind Management.

M = **Manage your thoughts.**

I   = **Initiate Action.**

N = **No Negativity.**

D = **Determine to add value to yourself and others.**

Scan the QR code below for a special video on mind management

CHAPTER 8

Turn Your Weaknesses Into Wins!

We all have certain weaknesses. Some of them are visible and some of them are invisible but we all have them. None of us like to focus on our weakness. We don't like to feel weak, act weak, or think weak. Have you ever gone on a job interview and the interviewer asks, "What are your weaknesses?" No! They are not really too concerned about your weaknesses. They are more concerned with your strengths and how you can add value to the organization. The interviewer does not want to hear your personal failures or some deep dark secret from your past that you failed at. Instead, what they really want to hear is a weakness that can be turned into a win. How can you turn your weakness into a win? First, we must acknowledge within ourselves that we have a weakness and we must be able to accurately identify it. If you do not know what your weaknesses are, you certainly cannot strengthen them. Nor do you have the ability to ascertain what your true strengthens are. Knowing your weakness helps you to understand and recognize your strengthens even more. Knowing your weakness will help you turn those very weaknesses into wins!

When I was younger I always thought because I was in a wheelchair and my weakness was obvious, that I was at a disadvantage. I thought that since my weakness was visible to the world that some people would try to use it against me. Throughout my life some people have tried to use my weakness against me but thus far they have been unsuccessful to crush my spirit. I have been overlooked many times for different job opportunities and promotions even though I had the qualifications. People tend to "see" the wheelchair before they "see" me. Knowing how people would under value me used to bother the heck out of me, it was a weakness for me. I have experienced and still experience people stereotyping me. They would say things like, "You don't work, do you?" As if it's impossible for a person in a wheelchair or with a disability to have a job, nonetheless be successful. People see me with my children and ask if they are my younger brothers. As if I'm not capable of having children because I am in a wheelchair. When I tell people that these tall, handsome young men are my children, they have this weird look of amazement and unbelief on their faces. All I can do is laugh. It's incredible to hear some of the things ignorant people will say. Many of us have been stereotyped at one point or another and it's not a good feeling.

****

Knowing your weaknesses will help you turn those very weaknesses into wins!

****

We live in a tough and cruel world and that is why I have made up my mind that I will not let this wheelchair define me, I will not let this wheelchair defeat me, and I will not let this wheelchair dictate my destiny. Where I have written the word wheelchair, I want you to say the sentence again but this time, add your weakness. You must first recognize your weakness in order to start winning. Here we go, say it out loud, I have made up my mind that:

I will not let this _____ *define me, I will not let this* _____ *defeat me, and I will not let this* _____ *dictate my destiny.*

I win every day because I never quit! It's hard to beat someone who never quits. I can't say, "It doesn't matter if I win or lose." That statement is not true. No one likes to lose, and we don't have to. Every day I wake up; I wake up with a mindset of winning.

I have used all of the stereotypes that people have placed on me and all of the judgments from people who have tried to disqualify me, as fuel to make me a better person. To make me the type of person that helps build people up and not tear them down. When we first started our company, I used to tell me wife Andrea that one day I would go from being *overlooked* to *overbooked*! As I began to network and meet different people, doors of opportunity began to open for me. When I first started my career in speaking, and I was trying to get more speaking engagements, we were sending a ton of emails and making a ton of phone calls. We even mailed over 50 speaker kits to different places, which cost us money, and you know what? We did not get one single phone call in return. The funny thing is that when I spoke to my mentor Willie Jolley about it, he said, "I bet you didn't get any callbacks right?" I said, No, I didn't! How did you know? He then proceeded to explain that in the beginning of his career, until his name became highly recognizable, he would often have to meet with people in person. It's easier to tell people face-to-face what you can offer them rather than just telling them over the phone. He also told me, no matter how many times they say no, keep trying. It's been said that usually by the 7th no, people will be so tired of saying no, that they will eventually say YES! Better yet, offer something so good that they can't say no to! The only option for them to say is YES!

****

I win every day because I never quit! It's hard to beat someone who never quits

****

I followed Willie's advice because it wasn't until I started going out in person to different places and meeting people face-to-face that things started to happen for me. I finally started getting some wins. It's amazing to see people's reactions and the level of respect you get when you look well dressed and you are well spoken. People will take you more seriously when you present yourself in a professional manor. Being able to meet people face to face was a huge plus for me because I was able to give people a visual of what they were going to get and what I was offering. It's very different meeting someone in a wheelchair who is well dressed, well spoken and a business owner, verses just speaking to them on the phone. I was able to share my story and experience with them in person. It *showed* people my passion and my ambition to make a difference in the lives of others.

I remember a time when I called a college over the phone to offer my services and the gentleman that answered said, Mr. Flores we get a lot of calls from people wanting to speak at our campus. They are all motivational speakers as well, can you please tell me what are some of the topics that you speak on? (In other words he wanted to know what set me apart from the rest.) I said of course; let me first start off by telling you that I am permanently in a wheelchair due to an illness I was born with. I immediately heard the change in his voice as he was now very interested in what I had to say. I proceeded to tell him what my illness was and how I was able to overcome many struggles. I told him what my topics were and that I also offered ½ day and full day workshops. He said WOW! That's great! Can you send me an email with more of your information? I was booked to speak at his college a few months later. The key here is that I used my weakness (being in a wheelchair) as a win. There are hundreds of people who do what I do. But there is only one of me, and only one of you. What makes you stand out? You may not be in a wheelchair but there IS something about you that is different! When you are seeking out opportunities, don't be like everyone else, find your weakness and turn it onto a WIN!

Maybe you are headed in the direction of your passion but you feel like you are at a dead end. You have to figure out who it is that you need to connect with and go see that individual in person. We live in a technology driven world and have technology at our fingertips. A simple Google search can tell you who in your immediate area is doing well in their field. Whatever it is that you aspire to become, start finding the people in your local area that might be able to help give you tips and advice and possibly help you take your dreams to the next level. Don't let your weaknesses hold you back.

There are some of us that allow our weaknesses to deprive us from living our lives to the fullest. Then there are others, such as myself who choose to use our weakness as a motivator to increase our strengths. I know that sounds cliché but it is so true. It took me years to realize that the very thing that was making me weak was going to be the very thing that I would use to help me become a winner. I have learned how to use my weakness as my strength to win in life. I have also learned to turn my weaknesses into consecutive wins and win several times throughout my day and so can you. No win is too small and no win is too big, a win is a win, no matter how you want to look at it.

Every time I get out of my bed and into my wheelchair to start my day, I win. When I get home at the end of the day after successfully tackling life, guess what, I win! When I finish a speaking engagement and somebody comes up to me afterwards and shares how my story or message has added value to them and has impacted them to learn more, do more, and become more, I win. Not only am I winning, but I am also helping somebody else to become a winner too and winning at his or her own game. Another big win for me was staying focused and finishing this book to make sure it got into your hands. That makes you and me a winner. It's a win-win for the both of us. Now when you are finished reading it, you can loan it or give it to someone else or better yet, you can buy one for someone else as a life-changing gift. When you do, you will be blessed because the winning streak will continue as it spreads to those around you.

For you it may be different because we all have different strengths and weaknesses. For some it may be choosing a healthier lifestyle if your weakness is food. You win when you choose healthier choices every day. For others it may be listening to uplifting music or watching positive TV shows. What you take in visually and by hearing, can affect your entire day, either in a negative or positive way. Or it may even be something as simple as turning off your cell phone for a while and spending some quality time with your loved ones. The examples can go on forever but the important thing is to realize what your weaknesses are and turn them into wins every day and win multiple times throughout the day. Every time you overcome any weakness, at any time, you become a winner.

****

Whatever it is that you aspire to become, start finding the people in your local area that might be able to help give you tips and advice and possibly help you take your dream to the next level

****

According to dictionary.com the definition of a habit is an *acquired behavior pattern regularly followed until it has become almost involuntary*. They say that it takes 21 days to develop a new habit or break an old one. I want to challenge you for the next 3 weeks to develop a habit of winning. Keep on doing it until winning becomes a regularly followed pattern in your life that becomes almost involuntary. Remember to recognize when a win occurs in your life. Remember to count it as a win and remember to celebrate each win along the way. Even if it's a small win, write it down, and celebrate that win throughout the day. Mentally acknowledge yourself as a winner because you did it. You made the right choices and decisions even if it's one decision at a time. Everything big at one time started out small. I believe in you, I know you can do it!

****

Every time you overcome any weakness, at any time, you become a winner

****

Winning has become a lifestyle for me and I hope that it will become a lifestyle for you too after reading this book. I believe that we were all created to win but many have been conditioned to lose. For some it may have been because of their upbringing. For others it may have been because of their environment. Either way, we cannot keep on using our past, our culture, or our lack of resources as excuses. We have to get rid of that type of thinking and become the champions that we are. I don't even think of losing anymore. I either win, or I learn. The key is to recognize what you have learned through the process so that the next time you are faced with the same challenge you can turn it into a win.

****

I either win, or I learn

****

Becoming a winner is something that is already inside of you just like weaknesses are also already inside of you. The one that you feed most is the one that matters. The one you feed most is the one that will dominate your life. It is possible for winning to become a habit in your life because after you win once, you now know how to do it again. All you need to do is keep following the same formula making minor tweaks along the way to win every chance you get. We are winners and we were created to win. Those gifts, dreams, talents, and passions inside of you were not given to you just because. No, God gave them to you to excel and use those very gifts to impact others to win.

Once you begin your winning streak the feeling is amazing and losing becomes less of an option. But keep in mind, when the losses come and believe me they do come, it's not as hard to recuperate from them. It's not as big of a hit when the losses do come because you have developed a habit of winning and you have been winning so well. Plus you already have your tailored made formula for winning that allows you to get right back on track quickly. You take the losses as "lessons learned" and move on. Every minute there is a new chance to win. Every day is a new day to conquer and win. What did you do today to win? Think about that for a moment and congratulate yourself if you were able to recognize and experience a win today. All wins, no matter how small, are victories. The best part is that the wins get bigger and bigger the more you overcome the small ones.

****

Keep following the same formula making minor tweaks along the way to win every chance you get

****

I took my family to the Dunn's River Falls a few years ago, in Jamaica. If you have ever been there, then you know that you start at the bottom of the river and you have to climb your way to the top. The amazing thing is that you are not taking the journey alone. There were people from all different walks of life; different cultures, different backgrounds, and different economical statuses locking arms and helping each other get to the top. It didn't matter where they were from because all they wanted to do was get to the top, win and be victorious. As I sat there, I thought to myself as I watched my wife, kids, and the others starting at the bottom and said, WOW! Look at all these people, arms locked, helping each other get to the top. It was an amazing experience to witness.

161

Most of them on their own would not have been able to make it to the top due to age, height and/or being out of shape. But thank God everyone was willing to help one another out and lend a hand. You could see it in their faces that they all had the same goal. We have to get to the top and we have to do it together! It reminded me of the saying, "No man left behind." I thought to myself, if we as a people could only do this in real life the results would be phenomenal! Now that is what I call a top-level achieving mentality! A mentality where everyone wants to get to the top, everyone wants to win, and everyone is helping others to win as well. I teach this very principle when I speak to corporations.

The only time we should ever be looking down on someone else is when we are reaching down to help them up. It's a win-win situation for everyone involved and all I want to do is see as many people as I possibly can win at life. The sad reality is that most people spend much of their time focusing and complaining about their weaknesses or their situation instead of their strengths and their futures. Make the decision today to choose to focus on winning and celebrating your wins and the wins of others. Keep a champion mindset; never count yourself out of the game, and keep on winning because the game is not over until you've won! I'll be rooting for you and cheering you on at the finish line. *Welcome to the winners circle!*

****

The best part is that the wins get bigger and bigger the more you overcome the small ones

****

Action Steps

<u>Turn Your Weaknesses Into Wins</u>

➢ *Have a champion mindset.*

➢ *Turn winning into a habit.*

➢ *Hang around other winners.*

➢ *Think positively and create a winning environment.*

Scan the QR code below for a special video on turning your weakness into wins

CHAPTER 9

The Power of Giving Back

If you wait until you can do everything for everybody, instead of something for somebody, you'll end up not doing anything for anybody." Malcolm Bane

I was raised and taught that it was always better to give than to receive. I'm pretty sure that many of you have heard that statement before as well. It's one of those things that can be easily said but not always easily done. Many people live with a mentality of scarcity. They think there is not enough to go around. The reason is that we often say to ourselves, well how can I give if I don't even have enough for myself? Or, how can I help or take care of someone else's needs if I can barely even help and take care of my own needs? Or, how can I help someone

165

else when I can't even take care of my own family? It is that scarcity mentality that keeps a lot of people from giving more freely because they think that the supply will run out. We could potentially end poverty, hunger, and homelessness if every single person just gave a little more? Think about that for a moment. If every single person in the world gave a little something extra (beyond what they thought they were capable of) we could eliminate this global issue and mentality of lack.

It was difficult for me to understand this principal of giving at first because we live in a world with a true "me" mentality. Everything is all about us. We are always asking ourselves, what can I get out of it? Or, what's in it for me, or what can I come up with to make sure I get ahead in life? We rarely think about other people's needs because we are too busy thinking about our own needs. It all boils down to a self-centered and selfish mentality that prevents some of us from giving out of the goodness and the abundance of our hearts.

I've heard many people say; when I have "enough" income coming in then I will be in a position to contribute financially. I was one of those people who always thought that giving had to do with some type of monetary amount.

166

Until I learned that there are many ways to give back that never have to do with money at all. Some of us go through life thinking that we have to be in a position of abundance before we are able to give anything to anyone. While having an abundance is always a great position to be in, it's not always necessary in most cases.

We can give of our time (which is a big one), our skills, or our talents. We can lend someone a hand and even our ears (which is also a big one) because some people just want to be heard. Another huge one that we probably do not think about, is so simple, and cost nothing, is giving thanks. Just giving a simple "thank you" to someone makes them feel appreciated and can also go a long way in receiving future help from the individual as well. There are several other ways that we can give without the need of money ever being involved. Money is not the only answer. If your *budget* (time budget, money budget, talent budget) does not allow for helping others then you've missed the point altogether.

I have seen many people at poverty level giving to others without any exchange of money what so ever. Like most of you, if not all, I would rather be in a position where I can give and not need to be on the receiving end. If you have ever given something to someone without any expectation of getting anything in return, then you know the feeling that you get by genuinely helping someone else who is in need. The feeling is out of this world. It gives you such a feeling of fulfillment and joy knowing that you were able to help someone else that really needed it.

A couple of times a year, my family and friends set time aside to deliver care packages to the homeless. Every time we're at the grocery store we pick up toothpaste, toothbrushes, female/male hygiene products, mouthwash, deodorant, combs, brushes, socks, and any hygiene related items that will fit in a gallon size zip lock bag. We call them Care Packages and we pass them out to over 200+ homeless men and women. The best part is that we don't just give out the care packages but we also show them that they are valued by speaking and spending time with them. We show that we care about them. We find out about their life stories, what they struggle with, and how they want to overcome. Over the years we have heard some amazing stories of adversity through their eyes.

One time, in particular, we were passing out care packages and getting to know everyone when my wife Andrea approaches a young woman and asks if she could give her a care package. The woman looked through the clear bag and noticed the comb. Immediately she started crying. My wife and I looked at each other in disbelief. Was this woman really crying over a comb? Not knowing the full extent of why she was crying, my wife asked her, "Are you okay? Why are you crying?" She then proceeded to tell us that she used to have long flowing hair but when she became homeless she had to cut it all off. She did not have a brush or a comb and with no real access for bathing, she had to eventually cut off her hair. As I looked up at her short bob cut, she said "I have short hair now and this comb is perfect! I can go to the public bathroom, wash my hair and now I will be able to comb it." She was so overwhelmed and my wife was now full of tears. Something as simple as a comb made a difference in that woman's life, even if it was just for a moment. We will not always know the effect we have on someone's life when we give back but know that whenever you do give, you have the opportunity to impact someone's life forever.

****

If your budget (time budget, money budget, talent budget) doesn't allow for helping others, then you've missed the point altogether

****

What did those care packages cost me? Well, it cost me time and money. But how much time and money compared to what I spent relatively? In comparison, it cost me very little. I allotted 3 hours of my time and 1 care package cost me a total of $5.00. Was it worth it? Yes! Would it have been worth it if I could only afford to give one care package? Yes! We limit what we do for others because we think that since we cannot contribute on a large scale that it won't make a difference. But imagine, just for a moment, you were the one giving that woman a package and she started crying over a comb. How would you feel? When we give of our time, money, talents, and resources, we keep ourselves humble. We keep our hearts selfless. Giving from your heart is the best place to give from anyway. Giving from any other place than from your heart means that you are just doing it for yourself.

Now I'm not saying to just give everything you have away or to do a service that you have provided to someone for free because we all need to make a living. What I am saying is that if you have the opportunity or you are in a position to give freely, it is better to do it without expecting anything in return because that is where the power of giving is found. It is found in our selfless acts of service where there is no expectation of a return involved. Please do not confuse the type of power that I am talking about. I am not talking about having an abusive or leveraging power over the person you are giving to, like saying "I gave this to you and now you owe me." No, rather I am talking about the power of the impact that you get to leave on the individual that you are giving to.

There is a special power that is released when they know that they do not have to pay you back or do anything in return for you. Just plain old giving with no strings attached. Now the funny thing is and I know you might find this a little cliché but there is truth to the phrase, "the more you give the more you receive". Now the question is, do we give more to receive more just for the purpose of receiving? The key is found in the reason you are giving, your motive. If you are giving from the heart for the purpose of giving then eventually you will receive because you have freely given. We will all reap what we sow right? So let us use the power of giving to bring light into a dark world. We all have the ability to brighten someone's day. Maybe it's to help someone with a new business because you've started a new business before, or maybe it's just saying a simple word of encouragement. Make it your purpose of give to others as part of your daily routine.

We will not always know the effect we have on someone's life when we give back but know that whenever you do give, you have the opportunity to impact someone's life forever

****

When I was fairly new into my speaking career, I was scheduled to speak at a Christian High School in front of about 400 students and faculty. My wife asked me if I was getting paid for this event and I told her that I had not spoken to them about my fee. I wanted to do it as a way of giving back to the community and that I was not expecting to receive anything from them for the event. After I was done speaking and shaking hands with the students and faculty I saw my wife packing up our camera equipment. I went over to see if she needed any help and she said, "Hey honey, the youth pastor needs you to sign this form because he is giving you a check for speaking today." I was a little shocked because the pastor and I had spoken over the phone a few times before the event and we never discussed any fees. I purposely did not bring up what my fee was during our conversation because I felt in my heart that I wanted to do it as a way to give back. I figured if they didn't bring it up then neither was I. And now the pastor was handing my wife a check for my services! Now that is the power of giving back my friends!

There are many of you who know exactly the type of power that I am talking about because you have already seen it or experienced it. But I know there are some of you who are probably thinking; can this whole power of giving back be true? Is this for real? I have given so much and I haven't seen anything happen in my life yet. Remember! Don't give up! Your harvest is on its way! Let your heart lead you and keep on giving as much as you can.

When you sow seeds you will reap a harvest in due season, if you don't give up. The key is *NOT* giving up. Not giving up on ourselves and not giving up on the people who need us. I want to encourage you to give from a cheerful and joyful heart and remember to give freely without expecting anything back. Die empty and give it your all in life because, at the end of the day when your time has come, you can't take anything with you. What you do get to leave behind is a legacy, an impact, and the

173

impression you have made in the lives of so many others that will last long after you are gone. I've heard it said that the world of the generous gets larger and LARGER. So make sure you sow generously so when the time comes to reap, you will also reap generously!

"We make a living by what we get; we make a life by what we give."– Winston Churchill.

As I write this book I am so overwhelmed that I am even doing it because I know the reality is, that one day, I will no longer be on this earth. So I decided to write this book so that my words will remain long after I am gone. A legacy and remnant left behind for my children, grandchildren, and everyone else that needs to hear them for generations and generations to come. This is also another way I am able to give back. I know I spoke about giving and not expecting anything in return but the only thing I do expect from you, is that you translate the information, stories, and experiences that I've provided to you in this book and turn it into action. Be the change that you want to see. You have the power to give back, start using it, and make a difference in as many lives as you can.

174

Action Steps

The Power of Giving Back

➢ *Give of your time just to listen.*

➢ *Volunteer your gifts and talents to help others.*

➢ *Give of your resources and finances if you are able to and when applicable.*

➢ *Partner with a charity or a non-profit organization.*

➢ *Whenever you give, give from a cheerful and a joyful heart.*

➢ *Give thanks!*

Another bonus value I want you to add to your belt of success and being Indispensable is the power of compassion. ***Compassion is one of those things that not everyone has, but everyone needs.***

I took my family on a Caribbean cruise and one of the ports of call was to Ocho Rios, Jamaica (this was our second time going there). Now if you were to know my family, you'll know that we go nonstop on vacation and try to explore as much as we can while on the islands. Most of the time, we try to find excursions and activities that are handicap accessible so that I can participate. Then there are other times when my family really wants to go on a specific excursion that is not accessible to me. Normally, I just stay in a neutral area and watch them from a distance. I don't mind doing this because it brings me joy to see my family having fun, being happy, and enjoying life together. Oh, how I wish I could participate in the fun and experience it with them.

In Ocho Rios, we went on an excursion to the Blue Hole. It's a natural spring in the mountains and at the bottom of the mountain there is a blue hole. It's as clear as drinking water. You can swim in it, jump off cliffs, and swing from the tree vines into the water. It's one of those breath-taking sights that you must see for yourself. As soon as we arrived, I was automatically looking for a neutral place for me to hang out because I knew this would be one of those excursions that I could not do, obviously because of the mountainous terrain. So I find a place that overlooks pretty much the whole area where I can still see my family having fun and take pictures of them.

As I'm sitting there watching my family get ready to start the trek, climb over these huge rocks and tree logs, one of the local tour guides came up to me and said, "Hey Mon, would you like to go into the water?" I looked at him for a moment like how do you suppose I do that? I guess he could read the look on my face because he said; "I will carry you on my back and put you into the water." So I looked around in amazement because I have been on plenty of vacations, to different places, and sure there are always people willing to help me but never to this magnitude. In order for me to get to the Blue Hole, he would have to carry me on his back through the mountain, over rocks, steep hills, and big tree barks to get me into the water. So I said to him, "If you are willing and able, then so am I!" So he put me on his back and we started the trek.

****

You have the power to give back, start using it and make a difference in the lives of others

****

While he carried me on his back there was another tour guide who carried my manual wheelchair for me just in case the guy who was carrying me needed a break. He could sit me in the wheelchair and take a rest if he needed to, but this guy took me all the way to the water without any rest and it was quite a distance away. I was surprised that he did not stop one time. We then arrived at the place where the water was a little calmer. He placed a life vest on me and sat me in the water. The water was freezing but felt so good. It was really hot outside and it's not often that I get to go into natural spring waters.

All the strangers that were there were watching in amazement as this guy carried me all the way into the water. They were all congratulating me on being so courageous by letting him carry me on his back to get into the water. He could have dropped me at any moment on the way but he didn't. He sat there with me and held on to me to make sure that the current did not take me away. I was there for about twenty minutes in the water watching my two boys, Elijah and Zion, swing from the vines of the trees and into the water. I watched as my wife, Andrea, jumped off this big cliff for the first time in her life into this amazing, beautiful, turquoise, clear water.

Now it was time for this guy to carry me all the way back up the mountain, over the rocks, and back to my electric wheelchair. I was so impressed by his ability and what stood out to me the most was that this guy did it with such joy. He was truly happy to help me and see me get into the water. You could tell he was authentic and genuinely wanted to help me have fun with my family.

When we got back on top of the mountain and he put me back in my wheelchair he looked at me and said: "You know you are the first person in a wheelchair to get into the water!" I said really! And he said "yeah mon" (which is a famous Jamaican saying) you did it! I then looked him straight in his eyes and said: "You have changed my life forever." I told him that God is good and said thank you so much for helping me." He said, "yeah mon anytime."

****
Compassion is one of those things that not everyone has, but everyone needs
****

That day was one of the best days of my life and I will never forget it. Do you want to know why? There was one man who decided to go above and way beyond to show compassion to help another man who couldn't help himself. He made such an impact on my life and the lives of my family. I'm sure he even made an impact with the strangers who witnessed him carrying me as well. We will always remember him for what he did. His name is Dev and we actually still keep in touch with him through Facebook to this day. Dev is Indispensable because had he not been there that day to help me, I would have never had the same experience. It was just one of those divine appointments that God orchestrates, behind the scenes, that you have to take advantage of and cease the moment.

One of our family mottos is "don't build things, build memories because they last longer!" The point here is, if you want to get to the place that you have always dreamed or wished of, you must be willing to take the journey. You must be willing to GO! It will take time, patience, dedication and commitment. If you are faithful to keep going, you will arrive at your desired destination. The excitement you will experience will be one of a kind! I promise you! If you are reading this book Dev, thank you for helping me to experience life, leaving a lifelong impact on my heart, and for being an Indispensable.

****

If you want to get to that place that you have always dreamed or wished of, you must be willing to take the journey

****

Action Steps

Being Compassionate Towards Others

➤ *Be willing to help others.*

➤ *Motivate and encourage other.*

➤ *Develop a heart of compassion.*

➤ *Be considerate and show empathy.*

➤ *Show kindness: kindness is contagious.*

➤ *Be patient with others situations and circumstances.*

➤ *Be sensitive towards others feelings and communicate in a warm way.*

Scan the QR code below for a special video about the power of giving back

CHAPTER 10

Don't Let Your Struggle Become Your Standard

In life struggles are inevitable. There are no ways to get rid of them but there are ways to face them, get through them, deal with them, and overcome them. We have all been through struggles at one point or another in life. Some of us have had financial struggles, physical and mental struggles while others have suffered through relational, emotional, and spiritual struggles and the list of struggles can go on and on. I personally believe that it is the way we handle the struggle that determines the outcome. We can either let the struggle become our standard or we can raise our standard and overcome it.

I believe too many people settle for the struggle instead of striving for success. The problem is that people get so comfortable with the struggle and so comfortable with the suffering that it becomes like a "normal" daily routine for them. Usually, because it's all they have ever known. For many, when they step outside of their comfort zone and break the routine it actually becomes uncomfortable for them. It is an unfamiliar territory and that frightens many people. So what do they do? They revert back to the struggle of pain and suffering because at least they know how to manage it inside of their "comfort zone."

The reality is that if you can break the routine of allowing the struggle to remain your standard and continue chasing after the life that you have always dreamed about, the struggle becomes less of a factor and more of an energizer. The struggle will actually begin to give you the energy you need to wake up every day with a hunger like never before. It is a hunger that drives you to chase your dreams, accomplish your goals, and tackle your ambitions. How many people do we know that have been struggling through life and have allowed that struggle to dominate them? How many have been stuck for so many years? You know the type of person I'm talking about. They have been parked in the same spot for years without ever trying to get out. The key is not even in the ignition, the lights are out, and they feel like they have run out of gas.

Maybe that person is you. Maybe you have been trying to figure it all out so you can get unstuck but nothing is really happening. If you've made it this far, I want to congratulate you because I know that the struggle isn't easy and obviously I know because I'm speaking from my own personal experiences. I want you to know that the victory is here and you can have it. All you need to do is put the key in the ignition, rev up the engine, and get ready for takeoff!

****

If you can break the routine of allowing the struggle to remain your standard and continue chasing after the life that you have always dreamed about, the struggle becomes less of a factor and more of an energizer

****

The word *struggle* by definition *is to try very hard to do, achieve, or deal with something that is difficult or causes problems.* There's no avoiding them, we all have them, and we all have to deal with struggles because if we don't then they will deal with us. You'll notice that I've

185

used several definitions throughout this book to give you the actual meaning of the words we use on a regular basis and in our everyday conversations without really knowing what they mean on a deeper level. We often do not realize the power of the words we are speaking. I believe that if we can have an increased level of knowledge, wisdom, and understanding of the words that we speak, then the more control we will have over what becomes our reality.

I mentioned earlier that when I was younger I thought that I would never be capable of doing anything great in life or do anything of significance that would make a great impact in this world. The story I was telling myself was the wrong one. I was definitely letting my struggles become my standard. I felt stuck, stagnant, and stranded. I'm glad that chapter in my life is over and that I had the chance to write a new chapter and a new story, the one that was the *true* story about me. The story about how I began to face my fears and overcome them. I decided to let the greatness inside of me out and I began to do great things. I said to myself, if those people were able to get theirs, then now it's time for me to get mine! Is it time for you to get yours? I believe it is!

I'm not saying that struggles will not be part of your life. There are some struggles that are temporary and some struggles that are permanent. What I am saying, however, is that you don't have to let your struggle become your standard. My struggle is a permanent one. I struggle every day of my life and my struggles are very real. The difference is that I have learned to face them, deal with them, and overcome them. They are no longer my standard. If you are not confined to a wheelchair then you can only think about the struggles I have to go through because you have never been through my struggle. The same is true that you may have struggles that I cannot relate to because I have never been through your struggle. One thing is clear; a struggle is a struggle regardless of the degree. Just because I am in a wheelchair doesn't make my struggle any more or less of a struggle than yours. No, struggle by definition is the same for everyone. Yet we often place our struggles in levels as if one is greater than the other. Folks, we all struggle but the real question is, what are we going to do to overcome that struggle?

****

If we can have an increased level of knowledge, wisdom, and understanding of the words that we speak, then the more control we will have over what becomes our reality

****

To give you a present day example of how real my struggle is, as I am writing this book, I took a short break to get some cookies out of my pantry. I was home alone and I wanted a little snack. I was able to extend my arm out as far as I could to grab the cookie box from the pantry. While I was bent over the side of my wheelchair with my arm extended, I put the cookie box on my lap. When I tried to push myself back to an upright position, the cookies slid off my lap and onto the floor. I was so upset! I had them right on my lap and then I dropped them. I couldn't even reach them anymore. Then I tried backing out of my pantry and the back wheel of my wheelchair got caught on the corner of the pantry door and I broke the top piece of the door. At this point, I was furious that all this was happening to me at the same time. First I dropped the cookies and then I broke the door. I started to cry because I was very frustrated with something as simple as trying to get some cookies out of the pantry and I couldn't even do it.

****
We all struggle but the real question is what are we going to do to overcome that struggle?
****

As soon as this cookie ordeal happened, I immediately started thinking about all the other things I could not do. I can't get dressed by myself or get into the shower by myself. I can't lift my arms above my head, I can't tie my own shoes, I can't cook my own meals and the "I cant's" can go on and on and on. I had to quickly learn how to stop focusing on the "cant's" because they were leading me nowhere fast. They were literally wearing me out. I had to re-train my brain to figure out ways to overcome my struggles and zero in on what I can do. What are some of your "cant's?" I really want you to understand that you do NOT have to let your struggle become your standard! I will say it over and over because I believe that you can turn your current life around for the positive and master anything you want for your future.

Since I told you about some of the things I can't do, let me share with you the things I CAN do. I can still brush my own teeth. I can still drive my own car with hand controls. I can still feed myself. I can still run my own company. I can still smile. I can still find the light when life is looking dark. I can love my wife and my children unconditionally. I can leave a positive impression with everyone I meet. I can motivate, encourage, and inspire others to learn more, do more, and become more. I can be a messenger of hope and help people to realize the greatness that is within them as well. I understand that life is a gift, and it offers us the privilege, opportunity, and responsibility to give something back by becoming more. When you become more you can then help others to become more by your teachings, stories, and experiences.

There will be times when you feel like you have what you want, right in your hands, or at least within reach and then suddenly it's gone. Just like that! In your mind, you're probably saying, "Great, what am I going to do now?" That is the question you have to ask yourself. What are you going to do when you thought you had what you wanted right in your hands and then all of a sudden it's gone and you are all by yourself? What are you going to do then? How are you going to handle that situation?

Are you going to let the struggle dominate your emotions, go into a rage, and take you off your path? Or are you going to refocus, regroup, and get right back on track? I cried for like five minutes and then I thought to myself, this is exactly why I have to write this book. I can use this book and my experiences as a tool and a resource to show millions of people that even though we all go through many struggles, some of them small and some of them big, we don't have to let it become our standard. I could have let this small mishap ruin my entire day and mope around depressed because of what happened to me and what I couldn't do.

Instead, I decided to shift my thinking and keep on writing so that I can share this fresh experience with you and empower you to continue with whatever your plan of success looks like, regardless of your shortcomings. We are all going to experience bumps along the way on our journey and its okay to have a five-minute breakdown once in a blue moon, but after that, you need to wipe away the tears and turn that anger into ammunition! Look through the scope again and continue to aim at your target.

****

Your character, your integrity, and your inner person are developed through the struggle

****

One of the keys to overcoming any struggle in life is learning to allow the things you can do outweigh the things you can't do. It takes a strong person to overcome any struggle, but your strength doesn't come from what you can do. It comes from overcoming the things you once thought you could not do. Focusing on what you can do will take you farther than you have ever imagined. Positive thinking always trumps negative thinking.

Your character, your integrity, and your inner person are developed through the struggle. I've been waiting a long time for someone to find a cure for the disease that I have. I have been waiting a long time for a miracle to manifest itself in my life through the grace of God. I have also recognized that what we learn and who we become in the process of waiting is even more important than what we are waiting for. Sometimes we just need to re-evaluate what we are focusing on. Struggles are evident in life but they don't have to remain relevant.

I also had to learn that the struggle is part of your story. It's what makes you great! It goes back to turning your weaknesses into wins. Your struggle is part of who you are. It is also part of the development process but it does not have to be part of who you want to become. The ironic thing is that you have to go through the struggle and get to the other side to become who it is you want to be. The real you is on the other side of the struggle.

****

Life is a gift and it offers us the privilege, opportunity, and responsibility to give something back by becoming more

****

The strange thing is that struggles are also required in order to survive in life. I know it's not what we want to hear but in order for you to stand up, you have to know what falling down feels like. You have to learn what overcoming the process of the struggle is like so when the struggles come into your life again, and you do fall down, you will also know how to get back up quickly. This book has provided you with many tools to overcome and never again allow your struggle to become your standard!

****

Struggles are evident in life but they don't have to remain relevant

****

Understanding and learning how to balance your life will help you tremendously. It's almost like a baby learning how to walk. They keep on falling and standing because of the imbalance, but once they learn how to balance themselves the less they fall. Then they learn how to run. That's when you better watch out! They're like little unstoppable machines that never run out of energy. In many ways, it is similar to us as adults. We need that same mentality that once we start running we become like unstoppable machines. Once we can learn to turn the struggle into an enduring energy that will sustain us (until we get to where it is we want to be in life) the struggle will not remain significant.

****

The real you is on the other side of the struggle

****

My hope is that you are now excited and motivated more than ever to live your best life now! You may not feel ready to move forward or things may not look perfect but start now! Start right where you are, with what you have, and watch your dreams unfold before your very eyes! I believe in you, but more importantly, I want you to believe in yourself and know that you are Absolutely Necessary and Indispensable Now!

"Strength and growth come only through continuous effort and struggle" - Napoleon Hill

"Don't let your struggle become your standard; let it become your strength"- Jose Flores

Action Steps

Overcome Your Struggles

- Let go of fear.

- Let go of your past.

- Focus on the positive.

- Refocus and Regroup as often as needed.

- Don't let the struggle become your standard.

- Rise above the struggle and soar like an eagle.

- Change the story you've been telling yourself and create a new amazing one.

Scan the QR code below for a special video on not letting your struggle become your standard.

Welcome to the family of Indispensables!